Student Development Theory in Higher Education

Moving beyond the theories traditionally used to describe college student development, this engaging book introduces social psychological theories that address the most relevant issues in higher education today. Covering theories and topics of ecological systems, sense of belonging, prejudice and discrimination, positive psychology, social capital, personality theory, mentoring, and hope theory, this book promotes the understanding and application of social psychological theories to various higher education contexts. Examples from diverse student populations encourage learners' application to situations in their own contexts. Comprehensive enough to be used as a main text but accessible enough to be used alongside another, this important textbook bridges research, theory, and practice to help practicing and aspiring higher education and student affairs professionals effectively work with college students.

Special features include:

- Reflective exercises that combine theory and practice and help students apply their knowledge to solve problems.
- Case studies and scenarios for further connections to the reader's university and college settings.
- Guiding questions that encourage students to think beyond the current literature and practice.
- List of further readings and references for readers to explore topics in more depth.

Terrell L. Strayhorn is Professor of Higher Education and Director of the Center for Higher Education Enterprise (CHEE) at The Ohio State University, USA.

Core Concepts in Higher Education
Series Editors: Edward P. St. John and Marybeth Gasman

Student Development Theory in Higher Education

A Social Psychological Approach

Terrell L. Strayhorn

NEW YORK AND LONDON

First published 2016
by Routledge
711 Third Avenue, New York, NY 10017

and by Routledge
2 Park Square, Milton Park, Abingdon, Oxon, OX14 4RN

Routledge is an imprint of the Taylor & Francis Group, an informa business

Library of Congress Cataloging-in-Publication Data
   Strayhorn, Terrell L., author.
Student development theory in higher education : a social psychological approach / Terrell L. Strayhorn.
      pages cm
   Includes bibliographical references and index.
   1. College student development programs.   2. College students—Psychology.   3. Social psychology.
4. Education, Higher—Psychological aspects.   I. Title.
      LB2343.4.S77   2016
      378.1'98—dc23
      2015018812

ISBN: 978-0-415-83662-3 (hbk)
ISBN: 978-0-415-83663-0 (pbk)
ISBN: 978-0-203-45821-1 (ebk)

Typeset in Minion
by Apex CoVantage, LLC

This book is dedicated to my parents, Wilber and Linda Strayhorn, my two children, Aliyah Brielle and Tionne Lamont Strayhorn, my grandparents who have all preceded me in death, and especially my maternal grandmother, the late Dr. Creola Evelyn Warner, who departed this life and entered eternal rest on November 23, 2013. My grandmother taught me to "love many, trust few," to dare to believe in the impossible, and to pay attention to all of life happening around me. Her life-borne wisdoms were my initial lessons in the importance of social psychology. And my kids and I are "people watchers" together today because she encouraged us to exoticize the ordinary, investigate the obvious, marvel in the mundane, and unpack the understood. I am eternally grateful for the many lessons she has left with us. I also dedicate this volume to my doctoral advisor and life mentor, Dr. Don Creamer, who nurtured my interest in theory and helped me learn how to use it.

CONTENTS

SERIES EDITOR FOREWORD

I met Terrell Strayhorn when he was a graduate student and I knew that there was something special about his way of communicating with audiences. He has a passion and way of connecting with people that is rare among academics. It is for that reason that I asked him to author a book titled *Student Development Theory in Higher Education: A Social Psychological Approach* for the Core Concepts in Higher Education Series.

Unlike many books on the topic of student development in higher education, this one is deeply rooted in psychology and it is also written with a sense of humanity and humor that compels the reader to want to know more and to move to action.

Strayhorn walks us through the various tenets of student development, while giving us examples that are vivid and real. He pulls us into his "silent movie" in which he watches and interprets the actions of others. For the first time since I read about student development theories in graduate school, they make sense in full.

Strayhorn also speaks to issues of race, class, sexuality—he demonstrates to us the intersectionality of students' development rather than ignoring these issues. Unlike scholars of the past, Strayhorn moves our understanding of student development into new territory and does not decouple the various aspects of student identity.

Given the continued interest in student development and the increased interest on student success in college, Strayhorn's work is sure to become a classic text in higher education and student affairs programs across the nation.

Marybeth Gasman, University of Pennsylvania
Series Co-Editor

PREFACE

Student Development Theory in Higher Education: A Social Psychological Approach was designed to fit the purpose and scope of the Core Concepts in Higher Education Series, co-edited by Ed St. John (Michigan) and Marybeth Gasman (Pennsylvania), published by Routledge. The purpose of this series is to provide books for major courses in the field of higher education and student affairs (HESA). The aim of the series is to produce 15 to 20 core texts that are used in the delivery of HESA programs. The publisher and co-editors assume that by creating a series of books that all have a similar voice, pedagogical features, and approach, student learning and outcomes can be enriched. And this is a perspective with which I strongly agree.

In 2011, the co-editors invited me to propose a core text focusing on promoting students' understanding and application of social psychological theories to higher education situations. Their original invitation emphasized that core texts should focus on synthesis of multiple studies rather than review of a single or narrow set of studies. The editors also stressed that core texts should be single- or co-authored rather than edited volumes (i.e., single editor but multiple chapter authors). And that understanding shaped the nature, scope, and contents of the current volume.

Three other factors influenced my approach to developing this book and its content. First, the author guidelines for the Core Concepts in Higher Education Series stated that the "main audience [for core texts] is master's students who need application of concepts, reflective questions, and other means to ground abstract knowledge." Thus, various learning strategies (e.g., reflective questions, recall exercises, vignettes) are embedded in the chapters that constitute this volume, affording readers multiple opportunities for making meaning of the material. Second, the guidelines also emphasized the editors' "desire [for] a balance between strong theory and concrete application." To this end, I include dozens of examples—sometimes parenthetical, sometimes not—throughout the theory sections of each chapter. For instance, when discussing self-efficacy as a theoretical concept that reflects the extent to which an individual feels capable/confident in his/her/hir ability to complete a task or function, a few everyday examples are offered that aid students in the consumption and application of relatively dense theoretical (and, at times, abstract) information. It's my hope that inclusion of such information satisfies the expectations of multiple audiences and demonstrates the appropriateness of the text for graduate student audiences targeted by the Core Concepts in Higher Education Series.

Lastly, when developing the proposal for this book, I spoke with 12 higher education faculty members (five of whom are higher education program directors) about the text, its scope and content, as well as courses for which it might serve as an appropriate textbook. Conversations averaged 35 minutes, ranging from approximately 20 to 50 minutes; the shortest conversation took place by phone with an "informant" sharing strong enthusiasm for the text, offering a few suggestions for topics to be covered, and encouraging me to submit the proposal to Routledge. Feedback from these conversations yielded three important conclusions that shaped the initial proposal and final product:

1. The proposed text meets a current need in higher education programs because no current text exists on this topic expressly;
2. The proposed text could serve as a primary or secondary core text for current course[s] in higher education graduate programs such as introductory theory courses, student development courses, research and theory seminars, and discipline-specific graduate seminars (e.g., Impact of College on Students, College Student Populations, Group Interventions);
3. The proposed text should cover topics that go beyond typical cognitive or psychosocial development theory to include topics that are frequently addressed in higher education (e.g., self-efficacy, social capital, prejudice) but whose theoretical origins lie in sociology, psychology, and related disciplines.

Drawing upon what I learned from the 12 interviews with faculty members, I worked with one of my graduate research associates to conduct a sort of meta-analysis of the social psychological theories employed in higher education research over the last 20 years, dating back to 1992. Specifically, we searched the top 4 most highly ranked serials in the HESA field: *Journal of College Student Development*, *Journal of Higher Education*, *Review of Higher Education*, and *Journal of Student Affairs Research & Practice*. Our analysis yielded eight interpretable topics (e.g., ecological systems, sense of belonging, social capital), as some were subsumed under other closely related concepts (e.g., racial microaggressions under prejudice, discrimination). These eight topics, then, became the focus of the substantive chapters in this book. Before describing the contents of each chapter, I explain the books primary purposes.

WHY WRITE THIS BOOK?

The book has several main purposes. First, the introductory chapter will describe the organization of the text, demonstrate the importance of this topic, and explain the approach taken when developing the text. Second, the book aims to synthesize, not merely review, empirical studies and theoretical information that relates to the chapter's primary focus. Literature will be synthesized in ways that draw bright lines of connection between the text and the relevant literature/theory from multiple disciplines. Synthesis of major theoretical threads and conceptual components will greatly enhance readers' understanding of social psychological concepts (e.g., prejudice, belonging); where possible, synthesized conceptual models will be outlined or presented graphically.

Third, the book employs several signature components to enhance pedagogical effectiveness and maximize students' learning and development. For instance, chapters include (a) summary material at the end of the chapter, (b) reflective exercises that combine theory and practice, (c) guiding questions, (d) case studies and hypothetical scenarios, (e) research tips, (f) further readings, (g) a list of references to information cited in the chapter, and (h) illustrations of conceptual models, where necessary. By introducing the text, synthesizing the relevant literature/theory, and including signature pedagogical components in every chapter, students' learning and mastery of the book's contents can be enriched, stimulated, and nurtured through engagement in educationally purposeful activities such as journaling, reflection, and critical thinking (Kuh, 2003). Prompts to do so are included in the book as well.

Please note that all names and people used throughout the book are pseudonyms and some institutions are fictitious names; any resemblance to real people or places is coincidental. While names and people are not real, as a way of protecting confidentiality and ensuring anonymity for past research subjects, the experiences they share, the insights they offer, and my interpretation of them are very real and add value to this book.

FOR WHOM WAS THIS BOOK WRITTEN?

Student Development Theory in Higher Education: A Social Psychological Approach was written with several audiences in mind. First, graduate students in higher education, educational administration, and college student affairs preparation programs might find the book useful for enhancing their understanding of theory, its relation to social phenomena that occur in educational settings, and the role they can play in promoting students' development using relevant theory and theory-based practices. Second, college student educators and student personnel, who work with students directly, should benefit from the detailed theory and research based findings presented in each chapter of the book. Such information may be helpful to them as they develop new or modify existing approaches for working with their students. Furthermore, campus administrators and college educators will likely find the practical recommendations provocative, useful, and possible to enact on their own campus. That the book focuses on students' experiences inside and outside the classroom should appeal to higher education professionals in academic affairs (e.g., provosts, deans, faculty) and student affairs (e.g., student activities, housing, recreation sports) and those who aspire to work in such functional areas. Fourth, the main substantive chapters synthesize findings from previous research studies that employ quantitative, qualitative, and/or mixed methods approaches; thus, educational researchers and scholars from related fields (e.g., psychology, sociology, gender studies, engineering) may be attracted to the book's empirical base, the various ways in which theory will be used to address problems or issues that frequently arise in higher education contexts, as well as the research tips included at the end of chapters.

Content included in *Student Development Theory in Higher Education: A Social Psychological Approach* makes it relevant for academic courses at both the undergraduate and graduate level. Specifically, faculty who teach undergraduate courses on human/student development, teaching and learning, or social psychological concepts might find the book an appropriate supplementary course text. Faculty at the graduate level who teach courses on student development theory, college student populations, impact of college on students, and even doctoral seminars on "special topics" might find the book suitable as a main course text, as recommended by program directors from select institutions. For instance, I teach a graduate-level course on college student development and a "special topics" seminar (Impact of College on Students) for PhD students at The Ohio State University—the proposed book would make a perfect primary or "core" text for both courses.

So, indeed, the book was written to appeal to a number of audiences, professionals associations, and college student educators. Three key features of the book include: (a) its comprehensiveness and scope [i.e., critical review of existing literature and chapters on various theories and subtopics], (b) its empirical base, and (c) its accessibility and recommendations. That is although the book draws upon an impressive literature/ theory base signature pedagogical elements are included along with sets of recommendations that are practical, effective, and hold promise for success in higher education and student affairs practice.

HOW THE TEXT RELATES TO THE CORE CONCEPTS SERIES

The text relates to the Core Concepts in Higher Education Series in at least three ways. First, there's sufficient evidence, from program directors, web searches, and existing standards, to suggest that this book could serve as a primary text for "major courses in the field of [HESA]." As previously mentioned, program directors shared that a number of them struggle to find a text that addresses a diversity of topics under a single cover. And the Council for the Advancement of Standards in Higher Education (CAS) includes such courses (e.g., student populations, impact of college, student development) in their list of "quality standards" for graduate preparation programs.

Another way the text relates to the Core Concepts in Higher Education Series is through its "focus on synthesis" rather than review of a single or narrow set of studies. Students will benefit from that synthesis while faculty might wish to assign specific readings in addition to the chapter that force students to read the original/primary source cited in one of the chapters. Lastly, the proposed text adopts multiple pedagogical techniques to facilitate students' understanding of material, encourage application of theory to practice and practical situations, and promote reflective thinking among students, which, in turn, can lead to enhanced learning.

HOW THE TEXT COMPARES WITH OTHER TITLES

Not only does the text compare to others in the Core Concepts Series, but it also can be compared with texts that some might perceive as its competitors. For example, informed readers will likely wonder how the text compares with *Student Development in College* published by Jossey-Bass. First, the present volume, *Student Development Theory in Higher Education: A Social Psychological Approach*, addresses a complementary and different set of theories. Jossey-Bass's student development book covers theories of student growth and development with a focus on psychosocial (e.g., Chickering), cognitive-structural (e.g., Perry), and social identity (e.g., Cass) theories. The present volume covers different theories ranging from social capital (Coleman) to prejudice (Allport), from sense of belonging (Strayhorn) to grit (Duckworth), to name a few, although references to foundational student development theories are included for easy cross-referencing of material and integration of multiple texts into a single course. The introduction of various pedagogical techniques in each chapter also distinguishes this text from others.

Readers may wonder if there are other volumes with which *Student Development Theory in Higher Education: A Social Psychological Approach* can be compared, one of which is *Social Psychology: Theories, Research, and Application* written by Professor Bob Feldman and published by McGraw-Hill in 1985. Offering a broad-based view of the field of social psychology, Feldman's outdated (and out of print) text covers a different set of theories from the current volume and, surprisingly, offers less than a handful of postsecondary examples in the 596-page tome. Feldman's book covered topics ranging from classical conditioning theory and interpersonal relations to social learning theory and behavioral norms. Again, the current volume covers different theories ranging from belonging to prejudice (Allport), from ecological systems theory (Bronfenbrenner) to capital (Bandura), to name a few, although references to other social psychology theories (through the use of shaded "call-out" boxes) are included where possible. It's important to note that several theories or social psychological concepts have been expanded or clarified by the original author since 1985—it's this new information that is included or referenced in this volume. Including various pedagogical techniques in each chapter that addresses a higher education issue or example also distinguishes this text from others such as the McGraw-Hill book.

It is my hope that this book will contribute to the body of knowledge in at least one of many ways. First, it might represent a worthy contribution to the national dialogue about theory in educational research. Second, it might be viewed as a powerfully useful tool or guide for undergraduate and graduate students, educational researchers, and faculty members who teach theory courses. Finally, if nothing else, I hope it begins to address some of the questions posed by my students over the use of theory in research—namely, what is it and how do you use it?

Keep in mind, gentle reader, that theoretical explanations are provided to render the complex, simple; realizing that a degree of accuracy is lost in the process. Indeed, this collection of theories is not exhaustive and was designed to provide a starting place for those who need assistance with understanding the role of social psychological theoretical frameworks in college student development. It is the first edition of many and it's a work in progress (as am I).

With these goals in mind, I release this volume to you.

Part I

Background of Theory

1

INTRODUCING . . . A SOCIAL PSYCHOLOGY APPROACH

Key Terms

belonging, collectivism, cognitive dissonance, evolution, individualism, neuroscience
self-esteem, social cognition, social psychology

INTRODUCTION

It's Tuesday. I just made it to one of my favorite coffee shops in the city that's open
24 hours a day, 7 days a week. I've come prepared for a day-long work session. Comfortable clothes, sporting blue Converse shoes. Lined note paper and stenographer notepads
chock-full of my handwritten notes and musing about the topic that is the focus of my
"day-long exercise." MacBook Air, all powered-up and ready to go. Free wireless internet
(no matter how intermittent it might be at busy, public coffee houses). And my magic
potion . . . coffee . . . in one of my favorite coffee mugs. By all accounts, I am ready to do
"good work," as I like to say.

As I take my seat at a brown table that seats four, though I'm going solo today,
I glance up furtively at the main entrance watching several other would-be good workers
pile into the coffee shop toting their bookbags, backpacks, and yes, 19-inch computer
monitors behind them. One woman, wearing red (one of my favorite colors), enters
slowly, moves in calculated swerves down the aisle of open tables, stops at every table for
a moment, closes her eyes, and pushes her chin up toward the ceiling, as if something
slipped her mind that would be etched across the ceiling above her. She did this continu-
ously. Table 1 . . . stops, closes eyes, looks up, turns head and moves on. Table 2 . . . stops,
same routine. Table 3 . . . stops, again, the same performance.

Just then two things occurred to me. First, contrary to what one might think, this
was not some new line dance that, in all its circulation, hadn't made it to Ohio yet. No.
And neither was she in search of forget-me-not reminders that were sketched on coffee
shop roofs or the backside of her eyelids. Actually she was trying to assess the volume

of noise surrounding each table by closing her eyes (i.e., removing any other visual distractions), tilting her head and ears up toward the ceiling where large Bose speakers had been mounted to amplify the coffee shop's playlist, and then looking around to see who would be her nearby neighbors and whether they were likely to have the same goals in mind—that is, more work than play and endless talking.

I had a second revelation from my time watching the young woman in red, who unknowingly had become the star in my silent movie: I'm a people watcher. And, in fact, I have spent a good portion of my life as a people watcher, personally and professionally. As a kid, I watched people all the time. Some might even call it staring, which adults always cautioned me to avoid. As a student, I often marveled at life happening around me and found wonder in watching people simply living. So much so that it influenced my choice of undergraduate majors: music and religious studies. Two seemingly disparate fields of study that, for me, are powerfully connected as they both serve as means through which people come to understand themselves, their feelings or emotions, and the world around them. It's little surprise, then, that I continue my search for understanding, for more "stars" in my silent movies as a professor of higher education who draws upon social psychological theories in my research. I am now and have for a long time been a people watcher. Are you?

WHAT IS SOCIAL PSYCHOLOGY?

Social psychology deploys scientific methods to understand and explain how the thoughts, feelings, and behaviors of individuals are influenced by the actual, imagined, or implied presence of others (Allport, 1985). While many other definitions exist, this is perhaps one of the most frequently cited and easy to apprehend. Building on this definition that shapes the scope of this book, let us consider a few examples.

First, how might the actual presence of others influence one's thoughts or behaviors? Consider Ben, a first-year White male college student whom I met during an evening diversity workshop that I conducted for a pair of resident assistants and their residents. After showing a short video clip about campus racism and affirmative action bans, I asked: "What can be done to promote diversity on college campuses like the one you attend, in light of information from the video?" Ben had been very engaged in the program and responded to several of my earlier prompts. He raised his hand quickly here too. I called on him: "Yes, Ben." He stuttered through his words but said: "I think it's an issue of letting go, you know . . . letting go of standards and high achievement criteria, you know, since the minorities aren't doing that well in high school or on the ACT and all. If you do that, then you can have more minorities, I suppose." Faced with wrinkled eyebrows, twisted mouths, long pauses, and hushed comments, Ben immediately recognized that he held an opinion that differed from others and, thus, abandoned his dissent, rescinded his previous offering, and joined the majority. Classic case where the actual presence of others influenced the thoughts, feelings, and behaviors of another.

Then what would it mean to be influenced by the imagined presence of others? Think back to when you were a kid. There were likely things that your parent(s) or guardian(s) asked you not to do. Don't go outside before you finish your homework. Don't stay up too late. Don't talk to strangers. And although they may not have been physically present when you were tempted to go outside before doing your chores or when you wanted to high-five the wanderer you met on the street corner, their imagined presence likely influenced your decisions. In fact, right now, you may still avoid speaking to strangers, consciously or subconsciously, due to the imagined presence of parents and other authority figures. A few years ago, I conducted a study of Black students in campus gospel choirs (Strayhorn, 2011). I met a young man whose mother passed while he was a freshman in college. Though deceased and, thus, physically not present, her imagined presence powerfully influenced the young man and motivated him to persist in college despite academic setbacks, emotional stresses, and his own willingness to quit. In short, imaginal figures can influence our actions by shaping our interpretation of events or the meaning we attach to them. And though imagined, their influence on our behaviors can be just as real as actual presences.

Finally, how can the implied presence of others influence an individual? Here, I offer an example from a participant in my national study of formerly incarcerated men of color who find their way to higher education (Strayhorn, Johnson, & Barrett, 2013). Several of the men in the study were first incarcerated at early ages (under 20) and over 50% were juvenile offenders. One shared a story about his habit of stealing. He loved to steal and could not understand why one would pay for that which could be stolen. He tried to explain where his self-proclaimed love for stealing came from and shared that "he didn't always steal." In fact, he used to be afraid of stealing, especially in stores with signs that read, "Under surveillance . . . you're being watched." The sign implied the presence of someone or someones who, though invisible to shoppers, was at all times aware of their actions, behaviors, and whereabouts. The implied presence of someone watching him influenced my participant's behavior and kept him from stealing. That is, until one day when he learned that some of those signs and the cosmetic surveillance cameras are just that . . . gimmicks to imply a presence that is neither real nor operable.

To recap, social psychology is an interdisciplinary field of study that attempts to understand and explain how the thoughts, feelings, and behavior of individuals are influenced by the actual, imagined, or implied presence of others (Aronson, Wilson, & Akert, 2010). Drawing on insights from multiple perspectives (e.g., sociology, anthropology, economics), social psychology attempts to gain a better understanding of the individual and how s/he/z fits into the larger social system. And it is this epistemological stance that informs my approach to discussing student development theory in this book.

IS SOCIAL PSYCHOLOGY SOCIOLOGY OR PSYCHOLOGY?

To deal with this question, let's talk about social psychologists or those academicians who see themselves as part of this discipline. From where do they derive their information and answers? Do they possess magic tools to make accurate judgments about social behaviors, free from error or the influences of so-called common knowledge? No, not at all. They, too, are prone to Type-1 and Type-2 errors such as failing to reject invalid hypotheses or rejecting those that may hold true. Yet, they specialize in using rigorous social research methods and theories to elicit data, findings, and other empirical evidence to support their assertions (Harman & Lehmiller, 2012). Full discussion of the methods they employ goes well beyond the scope of this volume; attention will be directed instead toward discussion of the theories that inform social psychology research.

You might be surprised to learn an interesting feature about the social psychology discipline that relates to the question that marks the beginning of this section. Actually there are two disciplines or subfields that comprise this area: psychological social psychology and sociological social psychology (Baumeister & Bushman, 2010). Psychological social psychology focuses on individuals and how they respond to social stimuli. Changes or differences in behaviors are assumed to be a function of people's interpretations of social stimuli, differences in personalities, or a mixture of emotions, which we've come to know as temperament (i.e., a stable estimate of one's nature that affects behavioral responses). Simply put, psychological social psychologists tend to emphasize processes at the individual-level and primarily use experiments to conduct their research.

Sociological social psychology intentionally minimizes the importance of individual differences and the influence of immediate social stimuli on human behavior. Instead, sociological social psychology turns attention to larger group-level or societal variables such as social roles, cultural norms, gender expectations, and social class, to name a few. Sociological social psychologists aim to explain societal-based problems such as deviance, poverty, crime, and, oh yes, educational disparity, achievement gaps, and belonging. They primarily use surveys, correlational studies, and observations to conduct their research, although the use of experiments is not completely uncommon (Haas, de Keijser, & Bruinsma, 2012; Steinberg & Piquero, 2010; Zanna & Olson, 2010).

Despite these disciplinary differences, most scholars in this domain identify as social psychologists. Two iconic examples that have relevance for those who work in higher education/students affairs include Leon Festinger and Kurt Lewin. The early years of social psychology were followed by what historians call a period of rapid expansion. One of the most significant lines of research during this period was Festinger's theory of cognitive dissonance. His theory posits that people's thoughts and behaviors are fueled, at least in part, by a desire to maintain cognitive consistency. Growth, however, is often the consequence of cognitive inconsistency, moments of disequilibrium that force individuals to acquire new information, try on different perspectives, or change their current opinion or position to restore equilibrium. Festinger's theory has been used in Sherry Watt's (2007) research on college students' engagement in difficult dialogues and the privilege identity exploration (PIE) model, as one example.

Kurt Lewin (1951) is best known for his work on topological psychology and field theory. A Jewish refugee from Nazi Germany, Lewin was instrumental in the development of the social psychology discipline. He firmly resisted pressures to decide whether social psychology was a pure versus applied science. His mantra was "No research without action, and no action without research," which some would argue as an early reference to today's "data-based" or "evidence-based" movement. Lewin once remarked, "There's nothing so practical as a good theory" (Schuh, Jones, Harper, & Associates, 2011, p. 135). And his theory ($B = f[P \times E]$) is the bedrock upon which our understanding of college student development is based. His theory suggests that behavior (B) is a function of the interaction (x) between the person (P) and their environment (E). So any analysis of social behavior must take into account aspects of the individual (e.g., traits), environment, and the interactions among them. His theory has been used to frame elements that are essential for promoting social justice awareness and action among college students (Lechuga, Clerc, & Howell, 2009).

So, in short, social psychology is neither sociology exclusively nor psychology exclusively, it is at all times a combination of both and more. Social psychology is interdisciplinary and deploys multiple methods in service to answering questions about social phenomena. As such, numerous higher education research studies adopt a social psychological approach to examine college student experiences, organizational or group behavior, and broad policy-related issues such as access, affordability, and campus racial climate.

WHAT HAVE WE LEARNED FROM SOCIAL PSYCHOLOGY?

The ultimate aim of social psychology, as I've said, is to better understand how the individual fits in the larger social system. So what, if anything, have we learned from social psychology research? And what does it have to do with higher education and student affairs? Consider the following findings from social psychology that may, at first glance, appear common knowledge:

1. Men exhibit more hostility toward women than women do toward men.
2. People who are paid a lot of money and work-related benefits to perform a boring task enjoy it much more than those who are paid little to no money.
3. To detect people's lies, you should pay close attention to their faces.
4. Physically attractive people are presumed more intelligent than those deemed physically unattractive.
5. The more bystanders there are to a crime or accident, the more likely a victim is to be helped or aided.
6. Students whose self-esteem is contingent upon their performance in academic tasks tend to feel "at home" and less anxious in challenging learning environments.
7. College students who feel as if they belong in college always perform better than those who "stick out" and do not feel as if they belong.

I bet you're thinking that all of these findings make intuitive sense and you can probably conjure up examples from your own life that resonate with each of them (especially #4 given the beauty amongst all of us in higher education . . . insert smile here).

So, why would an entire field or discipline be devoted to producing such obvious truths that likely can be informally attained? Well, for starters, because *all* of the statements above are generally *false*, invalid, lies even. The weight of empirical evidence from social psychological studies denies, disconfirms, and invalidates what's often assumed as "common knowledge" (for more about this term, see Figure 1.1). Social psychology research, to date, actually suggests the *opposite* of conclusions shown above (Dickerson, 2012). That's not to say that social psychology research doesn't also confirm many taken-for-granted notions about social behavior, but I think most will find that much of it challenges current beliefs that develop from everyday experiences and uncritical acceptance of other's thoughts, opinions, and views.

If not research, then from where did we derive most of our social beliefs? Naive psychology. That is, our everyday lived or observed experiences lead to naive theorizing about human behavior. For example, I have a colleague who works as dean of students

---

What's Common Knowledge, After All?

Have you ever used the phrase "common knowledge" to refer to some taken-for-granted truth or fact that's alleged to be so obvious that it needs no explanation or support? For instance, rich people have more money. Is this a valid and true statement? Any invitation for explanation is likely to seem fruitless or circular in thinking as most would just say, "Sure, that's common knowledge." A dog is a man's best friend. Why and on what basis? Again, here individuals are rarely compelled to produce generalizable evidence to support this claim. In fact, it's so pervasive that it shows up in media, social media, and casual conversations without introduction or defense. It's just "common knowledge."

    The term common knowledge was derived from David Hume's (1740) thoughts about the social nature of knowledge. Hume was perhaps the first to make reference to explicit knowledge and the importance of mutual knowledge (i.e., knowledge that's shared by many if not all). Yet, it was likely David Lewis (1969) who was first to offer an explicit analysis of "common knowledge," per se. And what we've learned from earlier works in sociology, psychology, and literacy studies is that common knowledge is important in social interactions, often assumed without critical analysis, and even common knowledge for some can be not-so-common for all. Interrogating common knowledge about social interactions, social behaviors, and beliefs is one of the primary goals of social psychology.

Figure 1.1

(DOS) at a small, Midwestern campus. She called me one day for advice about a student issue. Here's an excerpt of our conversation:

> **DOS friend:** I have a student here who's really struggling to adjust in her on-campus living situation. The other residents complain that she's withdrawn, overly quiet, and doesn't really participate in hall functions.
>
> **Me:** Interesting. So she's struggling to adjust, to fit in? Well, that doesn't make her unusual...many students struggle to find a sense of belonging in college. Why are you surprised about her?
>
> **DOS friend:** Because she's really involved on campus. She's like one of our most visible student leaders, I think, and she's always out in front doing things for the broader campus. So why wouldn't that be the same when she's at home in the dorm? You know?
>
> **Me:** Whoa, you said 'dorm'...is that allowed? (laughing) Yes, I definitely understand now. There's a common assumption that sense of belonging is a more global, general measure that determines students' educational success in all learning environments and that "fitting in" here will ensure "fitting in" over there, especially when we're talking about social spaces on the same campus. And while it's commonsensical, most of these assumptions are "false.com."

The conversation ensued and I "schooled" my DOS friend on college students' sense of belonging based on my own social psychology research in this area (Strayhorn, 2012). I explained that, contrary to popular [social] beliefs, sense of belonging is domain- and context-specific. For instance, one might find a sense of belonging on the university sports team as an athlete, but never feel as

> One can hardly deny that mankind has a common store of thoughts which is transmitted from one generation to another.
>
> —Gottlob Frege,
> "On Sense and Reference"

if they belong in their academic major. Think of football players majoring in organic chemistry and organic chemistry majors playing football; these are not necessarily synonymous. Sense of belonging is, in part, a consequence of the nature of relationships one has in certain spaces and negative relationships in a classroom might prevent facilitation of belonging, whereas positive relationships in a living-learning community might promote feelings of connectedness. Much more information about belonging is included in a later chapter; we'll return to this point then. My point, for now, is that while many casual experiences and observations might lead to what we call "common knowledge," social psychology research findings often challenge these beliefs, disconfirm pseudo-knowledge of this sort, and reveal new insights about social behaviors through a set of theories that provide a plausible explanation of the phenomenon under view. If you haven't already, go back and read Figure 1.1 before continuing to the next section.

ORGANIZING EXPLANATORY PRINCIPLES IN SOCIAL PSYCHOLOGY

The foremost organizing unit in social psychology is the individual and their interpretation of social situations. Though the discipline lacks a grand theory, social psychologists use five organizing principles in understanding social interactions (Gilbert, Fiske, & Lindzey, 2010). These are reviewed briefly in this section of the chapter.

1. The self is shaped by—and shapes—the social environment. This principle holds that individuals can be active agents in changing their own environment, perspective, opinion, or the nature of their relationships with others. For example, suppose a student, Gabriella, has devoted little time to studying weekly and has missed many more classes than she has attended, allowing her grades to slip from A's to C's and D's. One day during a morning jog, it dawns on her that if she continues in this pattern of academic underachievement, then she will not only get poor grades but may also be dismissed from college. Based on this interpretation of her situation and anticipated outcomes, Gabriella quickly revises her study schedule, devotes more time to homework, and starts attending class daily. She consciously (and swiftly) changes her behavior to avoid the negative consequences that she's able to forecast based on information from her present circumstance. This ability to study ourselves, analyze our own situations, appraise our surroundings and strengths, as well as our future possibilities enables us to shape and be shaped by the social environment.

2. Social cognition involves multiple strategies shaped by people's motives and needs. There's a long-standing debate in social psychology about the nature of human behavior. One perspective is that individuals are moved to act in hopes of satisfying their needs and desires, what is also known as affect. An alternative viewpoint holds that individuals act in response to a rational analysis of choices (or options) they face in particular situations, a sort of rational choice model. Advances in knowledge and technology led to the development of yet another perspective about social cognition. Social cognition refers to the way in which we interpret, analyze, recall, and use information about the social world. And social psychology holds that what people think will ultimately determine what people want, desire, feel, or are motivated to do.

3. Culture shapes social behavior. By culture, I mean the arts, customs, ideas, symbols, and material objects of a particular group, nation, or set of people. And if we can accept that social psychology is chiefly concerned with people's interpretation of social realities, then we must remember that people view the world differently, through different paradigms or worldviews, through different cultural lenses. One's cultural experience influences their take on reality, and thus, influences their social behavior. For example, let's consider cultural belief systems concerning the relation between individuals and groups, namely individualism and collectivism. In brief, individualism tends to prioritize individual needs over those of the group, whereas collectivism tends to prioritize group needs over those of individual members and emphasizes a willingness to submit to the influence of one's group.

To illustrate my point, let's imagine a college student, Terrance, who's faced with the decision to assume leadership as president of a campus club to which he has belonged as an active member for a few years. The president's role was vacated unexpectedly amidst rumors of academic dishonesty and fiscal mismanagement on the part of the previous leader. Members of the group nominate Terrance for his commitment, sense of responsibility, and capacity for collaboration. Terrance has never aspired to lead an organization, personally detests hierarchical leadership structures, and wanted to reduce his role in the group to free up time next year to study abroad. In the end, he accepts the nomination and, of course, wins the election, thereby giving up his desire to study abroad and avoid hierarchical power structures. Why? In an interview with a member of my research team, Terrance revealed that he felt compelled to meet the needs of the group even if that meant sacrificing his own needs and desires. Prioritizing group needs over one's own was something that he was taught as a young person and those collectivist beliefs were nurtured in him by his parents, grandparents, and church family (Strayhorn & Terrell, 2010). Indeed, culture shapes social behaviors.

ASSESSING YOUR CULTURAL PERSPECTIVE ACTIVITY

Collectivism or individualism—which one aligns more closely with your view of the world? Rank the list of values below in their order of importance to you with "1" being MOST IMPORTANT and "6" being LEAST IMPORTANT.

- Freedom and creativity, or latitude for open/imaginative thought _____
- Giving honor and showing respect for elders _____
- Independence, or choosing one's own goals _____
- Collegiality, or courteous interpersonal relations with others _____

- Pleasure, or fulfillment of desires _____
- Dependability, or state of being reliable and trustworthy _____

SCORING: To determine which cultural perspective seems to most closely align with your values, use the scoring rubric below to circle your top 3 values (i.e., those you ranked 1, 2, or 3). Whichever frame has the most circles is likely most reflective of your cultural perspective. Are you a collectivist or individualist?

KEY:

Individualism: 1, 3, 5
Collectivism: 2, 4, 6

Note: This activity was developed by the author using information derived from Franzoi's (2006) earlier volume on social psychology.

4. *Evolution shapes universal patterns of social behavior.* Though culture influences social behaviors, not all social behaviors are culturally constrained. Universal social behaviors have been presented in the literature and much of the discussion centers on how such patterns of behavior have evolved over time. Members of species with genetic traits best suited for survival in their current environment will produce more offspring and flourish, a process that Charles Darwin, a widely recognized biologist, called *natural selection.* As natural selection continues and the features necessary for survival change, the result is *evolution.* Evolution, then, is the gradual genetic changes that occur in a gene pool or population over time or generations. A long list of social behaviors studied by social psychologists are, or at least once were, thought to be shaped by inherent traits, including help-seeking, aggression, romantic attraction, and stereotyping, to name a few. Knowledge has advanced in most of these areas and some are less likely to accept them as universal behaviors; indeed, many social scientists are cautious in applying principles of evolution to contemporary human behavior (Conway & Schaller, 2002).

5. *Brain activity affects and is affected by social behavior.* Just as the evolutionary perspective comes from the field of biology, so too does a new subfield within social psychology that explores connections between social processes and neural processes of the brain: social neuroscience or brain activity. Social neuroscience emphasizes the reciprocal relationship between these two—that is, how the brain influences social interactions and behaviors, as well as how social interactions might influence the brain. Although much of this goes beyond the scope of this text and the theories discussed in subsequent chapters, I firmly believe that it remains a central organizing principle of social psychological explanations.

Much of the work in this area has to do with highly technical terms and medical techniques—such as brain-imaging techniques or functional magnetic resonance imaging (MRI)—that measure, plot, or map the brain's metabolic activity by region. Higher education studies rarely use this principle extensively, although there are published studies based on college students. For example, Hajcak, McDonald, and Simons (2003) studied neural processes—specifically error-related negativity (ERN)—observed in college students with obsessive-compulsive disorder. Results showed that subjects high in anxiety and worry have greater ERN brain activity than control subjects with little to no worry or anxiety. As another example, Zeigler et al. (2005) found that underage alcohol use and abuse is positively associated with brain damage and neurodegeneration (i.e., deficits), particularly in regions responsible for learning and memory. Take home message? College students should be anxious in nothing; don't worry, be happy; and use alcohol responsibly, if at all. Simple, right? Easily said, yet much more difficult to mount on college campuses. Fortunately, the scope of this book does not require full discussion of this point or empirically based strategies for ridding American campuses of excessive alcohol consumption. Rather it's enough to say that brain activity affects and is affected by social behavior, which is one of the more recent guiding principles of social psychology.

CONCLUSION

As you can see, social psychology connects to many other areas of inquiry and the field has grown over the years in terms of its literature, methods, and theories. A social psychological approach provides greater insights into social processes and realities than other approaches that are based in single disciplines or individual techniques. This introductory chapter serves as a foundation or primer, as it were, for those new to the study of social psychology theories in higher education. The remaining chapters in this text will provide you with useful information, fascinating insights, and provocative conclusions about not only college student development but also about you, gentle reader, and your social world. To me, that's the beauty of social psychology— it reveals much about the social world and the more you learn about social interactions, the more you learn about yourself, the world around you, and how you can more effectively move within it. Complete the reflective exercises below before continuing to the next chapter. Then, turn the page and let's begin the discussion of relevant theories.

REFLECTIVE EXERCISES

1. Define "social psychology" in your own words.
2. Name at least one social psychologist whose research is relevant to higher education, student affairs, or our understanding of college student development.
3. Critically assess the veracity of this statement using information from this chapter or insights gleaned from your other graduate courses. "Once a student finds a sense of belonging on campus, they're guaranteed to succeed in college."
4. Think back to the story of "Terrance," who was nominated by his peers to lead a campus club, in an earlier section of this chapter. His story served as an example of how individualism and collectivism—cultural perspectives on human relations—can influence student behaviors. Can you think of other examples of ways in which culture influences student behaviors, decisions, or responses? Describe at least one instance from your work with students or what you've learned from other courses.
5. Recall Kurt Lewin's social psychological theory about social behaviors. What's the formula? What does it mean? And how does it apply to your work with college students? Offer at least two examples.

CHAPTER SUMMARY

1. The self is a central, organizing concept in social psychology.
2. Social psychology actually is composed of two disciplines or subfields: sociological social psychology and psychological social psychology; one emphasizes social interactions at the group or macro-level while the other focuses on the individual-level, respectively.
3. Psychological social psychologists tend to use experimental designs, while their sociology counterparts use surveys, observations, and correlational designs more frequently.
4. Social psychology, among many other things, interrogates "common knowledge" using scientific methods and substantive theories about social processes and human relations.
5. Five organizing principles of social psychology include: (a) the self is shaped by—and shapes—the social environment, (b) social cognition involves multiple cognitive strategies shaped by one's motives and needs, (c) culture shapes social behavior, (d) evolution shapes universal patterns of social behavior, and (e) brain activity affects and is affected by social behavior.

DEFINITIONS

Working back through the chapter, develop a working definition of the following list of terms that relate to the study of social psychology and college student development theory.

- belonging
- collectivism
- common knowledge
- cognitive dissonance
- culture
- evolution
- individualism
- naive psychology
- neuroscience
- self-esteem
- social cognition
- social psychology

RESEARCH TIPS

1. Psychological social psychologists tend to employ experimental designs in their research.
2. Sociological social psychologists tend to employ correlational designs, surveys, and observations in their research.
3. Mixed methods, whether sequential, concurrent, or otherwise ordered, have significant potential for use in social psychology research. Readers are encouraged to consider the appropriate use of blended methods in studies of social interactions.

4. Experimental and quasi-experimental designs require use of rigorously developed experimental and control groups. Generally, "experimental" refers to a group of subjects who have received treatment, intervention, or exposure to the condition under study; "controlled" groups are composed of individuals who have been denied treatment, avoided intervention, or somehow kept from exposure to the condition. For more about experimental designs in education research, consult Schneider et al. (2007).

5. The rigor of correlational designs and other survey-based studies is enhanced through the use of strong theory, reliable, and valid instruments (or scales), sophisticated statistical techniques appropriate for the question under study, and statistical controls (where necessary) that subtract the effect of confounding factors on the key dependent variable(s).

FURTHER READING

Allport, G.W. (1985). The historical background of social psychology. In G. Lindzey & E. Aronson (Eds.), *Handbook of social psychology* (Vol. 1, pp. 1–46).

Aronson, E., Wilson, T.D., & Akert, R.M. (2010). *Social psychology* (7th ed.). Upper Saddle River, NJ: Prentice Hall.

Baumeister, R.F., & Bushman, B.J. (2010). *Social psychology and human nature* (2nd ed.). Belmont, CA: Thomson/Wadsworth.

Dickerson, P. (2012). *Social psychology: Traditional and critical perspectives*. Harlow: Pearson.

Gilbert, D.T., Fiske, S.T., & Lindzey, G. (Eds.). (2010). *Handbook of social psychology* (5th ed.). New York: Wiley.

Harman, J.J., & Lehmiller, J.J. (2012). *A social psychology research experience*. San Diego, CA: Cognella.

Zanna, M., & Olson, J.M. (Eds.). (2010). *Advances in experimental social psychology* (Vol. 43). San Diego, CA: Academic Press.

REFERENCES

Allport, G.W. (1985). The historical background of social psychology. In G. Lindzey & E. Aronson (Eds.), *Handbook of social psychology* (Vol. 1, pp. 1–46).

Aronson, E., Wilson, T.D., & Akert, R.M. (2010). *Social psychology* (7th ed.). Upper Saddle River, NJ: Prentice Hall.

Baumeister, R.F., & Bushman, B.J. (2010). *Social psychology and human nature* (2nd ed.). Belmont, CA: Thomson/Wadsworth.

Conway, L.G., & Schaller, M. (2002). On the verifiability of evolutionary psychological theories: An analysis of the psychology of scientific persuasion. *Personality and Social Psychology Review, 6,* 152–160.

Dickerson, P. (2012). *Social psychology: Traditional and critical perspectives*. Harlow: Pearson.

Franzoi, S.L. (2006). *Social psychology* (4th ed.). New York: McGraw-Hill.

Frege, G. (1980). On sense and reference. (M. Black, Trans.). In P. Geach & M. Black (Eds. And Trans.), *Translations from the philosophical writings of Gottlob Frege*. Oxford: Blackwell. (Original work published 1892)

Gilbert, D.T., Fiske, S.T., & Lindzey, G. (Eds.). (2010). *Handbook of social psychology* (5th ed.). New York: Wiley.

Haas, N.E., de Keijser, J.W., & Bruinsma, G.J.N. (2012). Public support for vigilantism: An experimental study. *Journal of Experimental Criminology, 8,* 387–413.

Hajcak, G., McDonald, N., & Simons, R.F. (2003). Anxiety and error-related brain activity. *Biological Psychology, 64*(1–2), 77–90.

Harman, J.J., & Lehmiller, J.J. (2012). *A social psychology research experience*. San Diego, CA: Cognella.

Hume, D. (1740). *A treatise of human nature* (2nd ed.). Oxford: Claredon Press.

Lechuga, V.M., Clerc, L.N., & Howell, A.K. (2009). Power, privilege, and learning: Facilitating encountered situations to promore social justice. *Journal of College Student Development, 50*(2), 229–244.

Lewin, K. (1951). *Field theory in social science*. New York: Harper.

Lewis, D. (1969). *Convention: A philosophical study*. Cambridge, MA: Harvard University Press.

Schneider, B., Carnoy, M., Kilpatrick, J., Schmidt, W.H., & Shavelson, R.J. (2007). *Estimating causal effects using experimental and observational designs*. Washington, DC: American Educational Research Association.

Schuh, J.H., Jones, S.R., Harper, S.R., & Associates (Eds.). (2011). *Student services: A handbook for the profession* (5th ed.). San Francisco, CA: Jossey-Bass.

Steinberg, L., & Piquero, A. R. (2010). Manipulating public opinion about trying juveniles as adults: An experimental study. *Crime & Delinquency, 56*(4), 487–506.

Strayhorn, T. L. (2011). Singing in a foreign land: An exploratory study of gospel choir participation among African American undergraduates at a predominantly White institution. *Journal of College Student Development, 52*(5), 137–153.

Strayhorn, T. L. (2012). *College students' sense of belonging: A key to educational success.* New York: Routledge.

Strayhorn, T. L., Johnson, R. M., & Barrett, B. A. (2013). Investigating the college adjustment and transition experiences of formerly incarcerated Black male collegians at predominantly White institutions. *Spectrum: A Journal on Black Men, 2*(1), 73–98.

Strayhorn, T. L., & Terrell, M. C. (Eds.). (2010). *The evolving challenges of Black college students: New insights for policy, practice, and research.* Sterling, VA: Stylus.

Watt, S. K. (2007). Difficult dialogues, privilege and social justice: Uses of the privileged identity exploration (PIE) model in student affairs practice. *College Student Affairs Journal, 26*(2), 114–126.

Zanna, M., & Olson, J. M. (Eds.). (2010). *Advances in experimental social psychology* (Vol. 43). San Diego, CA: Academic Press.

Zeigler, D. W., Wang, C. C., Yoast, R. A., Dickinson, B. D., McCaffree, M. A., Robinowitz, C. B., & Sterling, M. L. (2005). The neurocognitive effects of alcohol on adolescents and college students. *Preventive Medicine, 40*(1), 23–32.

2

WHAT'S THEORY ANYWAY?

If the facts don't fit the theory, change the facts.

—Albert Einstein

Experience without theory is blind, but theory without experience is mere intellectual play.

—Immanuel Kant

Key Terms

Chickering's vectors, cognitive dissonance, development, framework, maturation, Perry's positions, theory

INTRODUCTION

Cognitive science has shown that the human mind best understands myriad facts when they are organized into a conceptual map, narrative (see chapter 9 on "Hope Theory" in this volume), mental map, illustrative diagram, or intuitive theory. Theory is generally defined as a plausible explanation of an observed phenomenon. And, in higher education, theory offers a fairly elaborate explanation or hypothesis for observed phenomena such as attrition, intellectual development, identity formation, socialization, and sense of belonging, to name a few. It provides educators with knowledge about how learning occurs that can be used to create effective interventions designed to increase learning and development (Strayhorn, 2013a).

Theory is one term with many definitions. It is often confused with hypothesis, conjecture, and hunch. But theory is much more than a guess. Theory also has been qualified by adjectives like minor (theory), emergent (theory), and grand theory. As Kerlinger (1986) explained, theory is defined as "a set of interrelated constructs, definitions, and propositions that presents a systematic view of phenomena by specifying relations among variables, with the purpose of explaining and predicting phenomena" (p. 9).

Generally, I use the term theory to refer to plausible explanations of observed phenomena (Strayhorn, 2006, 2013a), and in higher education these phenomena usually occur on campus, in college, during the "college years," or perhaps earlier in life with an influence on one's college experience. For instance, many higher education students will be familiar with Chickering's (1969) theory that proposes seven vectors of development that lead to establishing one's identity: developing competence, managing emotions, moving through autonomy toward interdependence, developing mature interpersonal relationships, establishing identity, developing purpose, and developing integrity. His model centers principally on identity development during the college years (Strayhorn, 2006).

As another example, researchers in higher education often employ or augment existing theories with notions borrowed from other fields and disciplines such as sociology (Strayhorn, 2013a); a common example of this is higher education's use of human, social, and cultural capital theories, which I have referred to collectively as sociocultural theory (Strayhorn, 2008). Human capital theory posits that individuals make investments in education or training to gain additional knowledge, skills, and abilities that are often associated with monetary and non-monetary benefits such as increased income or occupational status, respectively. While human capital refers to the "information, knowledge, skills, and abilities of an individual that can be exchanged in the labor market for returns such as salary, financial rewards, and jobs" (Strayhorn, 2008, p. 31), social capital refers to the information-sharing networks or instrumental, supportive relationships that an individual may have that provide access to information and opportunity. And cultural capital is the system of beliefs, tastes, and preferences derived from one's parents or guardians that typically define one's class standing (Bourdieu, 1997).

It is generally assumed that the more education an individual attains, the more human capital one accumulates and, thus, the more benefits one accrues. Productive social networks yield capital that makes possible the achievement of certain goals that in its absence would not be possible (Coleman, 1988). And quite often people activate their social capital to acquire the cultural capital necessary to succeed in college—this is a widely accepted underlying explanation for why continuing generation college students outperform their first-generation counterparts (Pascarella & Terenzini, 2005). If higher education researchers can borrow from sociology to expand the power of their theories to explain college phenomena, then it should be clear how social psychological perspectives can be used to do the same. This is the approach that informs the present volume.

Just as theory has many published definitions, there are a number of metaphors that can be used to signal the role that it plays in social science. For instance, I presented elsewhere (Strayhorn, 2013a) what I find to be a confusing array of terms used to allude to theory, such as conceptual frames (Merriam, 1998); propositions (Argyris & Schon, 1974); abstract categories (LeCompte & Preissle, 1993); conceptual maps (Ausubel, 1963); stances (Crotty, 1998); and postulations (Astin, 1984), to name a few. There are other metaphors, such as framework, lens, and one of my favorites, glue, that capture the essence of theory in social fields. These are discussed in the next section.

Two caveats about theory's role before we move beyond mere definitions of the term. Theory is a powerful tool . . . no doubt. But every theory has limits. Where one theory helps us see something that might otherwise go unnoticed, it may simultaneously conceal other aspects of the phenomena. All theories have virtues and limits. Knowing a theory, its core elements, key concepts, and how it has been used in previous research (on its own or with other theories) greatly enriches one's ability to deploy the theory in their own work. This drove my decision to organize each chapter of this book around these major headings.

It's also true that theory, by definition, aims to make the complex simple, realizing that any attempt to render sophistications as simple gives up a degree of accuracy in exchange for simplicity and sometimes accessibility; this is the paradox of theory. And although we often refer to it as theory, explanation, framework, or "theoretical model," constructions of college's impact on students such as Astin's (1991) input–environment–outcome (I-E-O) model are less of an attempt to explain the underlying causal mechanism—the "how and why"—of students' development than a conceptual guide to enable or enrich our understanding of college students, their experiences, and our relations with them (Pascarella & Terenzini, 2005). Readers of this volume are encouraged to keep these caveats in mind when consuming the book's content.

QUOTABLE MOMENT

If you have built castles in the air, your work need not be lost; that is where they should be. Now put the foundation under them.

—Henry David Thoreau, *Walden Pond*

Just as Thoreau encourages one to put a foundation under castles built in the air, students should use theory to support emergent ideas.

THEORY AS FRAMEWORK

Most dictionaries define framework as a skeletal structure that's designed to support or undergird something. Framework also refers to an essential support structure underlying a system or concept. That is, a framework provides essential or necessary support that's impossible, improbable, or at least, unwise to go without. This is a powerful metaphor for thinking about the role theory plays in our work with students. Figure 2.1 presents a list of common metaphors.

Another way framework applies to our discussion of theory is in terms of higher-order connections. Imagine the builder who constructs a large edifice; it's the nuts, bolts, braces, and columns of the structure that connect "ground zero" to higher floors. Applied to higher education this may reflect disconnects between theory and practice, individualization and generalizability. Some higher education professionals spend so much time on "ground zero" in the trenches, so to speak, or "on the frontline" of service that they become so local in their orientation to a problem that generalization (or view of higher floors) is virtually impossible. They miss the forest for the trees. This local orientation to a problem prevents personnel from seeing larger issues, trends, or public goods and all-too-often result in doing "just enough for now" or "to get by" versus fixing the deeper problem. As framework, theory can provide the scaffolding necessary to link a topic, concern, or ordinary student meeting to a critical, looming issue in higher education. In this way, theory helps one build hierarchical connections between otherwise discon-nected, distant, or different parts. Like nuts, bolts, and beams help to connect the bottom floor (ground zero) of a building to the highest floor, so too does theory help to connect single stories to larger understandings. See Figure 2.2 for more.

While metaphors like framework are powerful devices for aiding understanding of the-ory's role in research, the term can be misleading and blur meaning. For instance, theory can help frame an educational problem or provide very useful insights for understanding

Theory	Model
Framework	Hypothesis
Lens	Conjecture
Glue	Tool
Perspective	Worldview

Figure 2.1 A list of theory metaphors

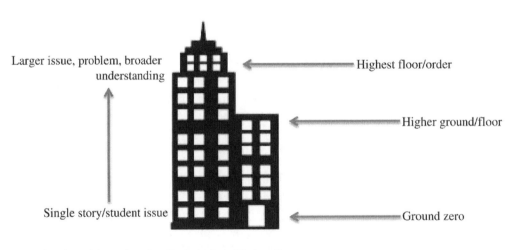

Note. Photo is stock image from freepik.com in the public domain.

Figure 2.2 Theory as scaffolding for building hierarchical connections

how identity development may unfold for some individuals, under certain conditions, at particular phases of life. But identity development frames are not essential in the sense of applying equally well to all (Strayhorn, 2013b). We've known for years now that identity development looks different for majority students, ethnic minorities, Black Americans, and lesbian, gay, bisexual, and transgendered students (Chickering, 1969; Cross, 1971; D'Augelli, 1991; Phinney, 1990), to name a few. Readers are urged not to interpret theory as framework in this way. Rarely, if ever, does one theory fit all.

THEORY AS NECESSARY FRAMEWORK

Theory can be described as framework and we just discussed framework as essential or necessary support that's unwise to go without. Going without theory in higher education would be like building a skyscraper without the steel braces, columns, and beams that equip the behemoth to withstand enormous weight. Interestingly, all engineering and architecture majors will recall that the forces that act on structures are called "loads." Without the necessary framework, a tall skyscraper would buckle under pressure of a heavy load. Framework is essential and necessary in both construction and higher education practice.

1. In your opinion, how is theory essential to your work with college students?
2. Can you recall a time when theory was essential or necessary to your work in higher education? Describe the time with sufficient details about who, what, when, where, and how theory played a role.
3. If theory is framework and framework equips a building to withstand the pressure of heavy loads, then how do college student educators use theory to equip college students to withstand forces that act upon them? For instance, how might theory empower a socially alienated student to find their way to belonging? Share your responses with others.

THEORY AS LENS

Theory allows us to "see" that which might otherwise go hidden, concealed, or too blurry to be captured with clarity. Theory can be applied for sense making, as a sort of spectacle for viewing things—usually social phenomena—as they are. In this way, theory acts as lens.

Anyone who wears glasses or knows someone who views the world through corrective lenses can likely relate to this example. It's the usual eye exam. Optometrist enters the room, places you behind a computerized machine, and flips through various lens combinations, each rendering the distant line of letters more or less legible. "Is this better, worse, or about the same?," the OD (doctor of optometry) asks, flipping slowly between ocular setting "1" and "2." Lest you say "about the same," the exam continues with the OD offering a different combination for comparison. "Now, is this better, worse, or about the same?" The goal of this exercise is to identify the best set of lenses that offer optimal visual clarity to the patient who affirms the OD's prescription by reciting: "S C T H L N Y" (the last and usually smallest line of letters displayed on the examining wall).

THE POWER OF EXPERIENCE

If you want to know the taste of a pear, you must change the pear by eating it yourself. If you want to know the theory and methods of revolution, you must take part in revolution. All genuine knowledge originates in direct experience.

—Mao Zedong

All genuine education comes about through experience. . . .

—John Dewey

Similar wisdom holds for theory as a lens. Here theory serves as an instrument for viewing something with acuity and a degree of clarity that's only possible with the theory's aid. For instance, a historic purpose of higher education is to foster intellectual development of students. But what does that mean—intellectual development? It's difficult to foster or promote something you hardly understand. (Think about individuals who hope to increase their credit score but have no knowledge of how credit scores are calculated, reported, or influenced by liens, repossessions, or credit history inquiries. Without some understanding, any attempt is likely fruitless.)

A corpus of studies has posited that students grow and change cognitively in varied and complex ways. One example of a cognitive-structural theory is Perry's (1968) intellectual development model. Perry described nine positions that can be grouped into four categories: (a) dualism, (b) multiplicity, (c) relativism, and (d) commitment. His theory simplifies intellectual development (a complex phenomenon on its own) to a logical progression from simple, binary meanings to more complex, nuanced modes of reasoning. Without theory, intellectual development might be dismissed as too complex for apprehension . . . or in OD language, ocular setting #1. With theory, intellectual development can be viewed or "seen" as movement from simple to complex ways of knowing, cognitive shifts from dualism to commitment, or accepting the possibility of multiple realities and multiple authoritative sources of knowledge (including self as producer of knowledge) . . . akin to ocular setting #2. So, which is better, worse, or are they about the same? 1 or 2? Clearly, 2 is better. That's theory as lens.

One of the benefits of using theory as lens or perspective is that one can arrive at very different images based on the theory in hand. For instance, an academic advisor who examines a student's infrequent class attendance through Tinto's (1993) attrition lens may attribute this behavior to a lack of goal or institutional commitment. The same academic advisor, or another, could view the same symptoms through a belonging lens (Strayhorn, 2012) and attribute college-level truancy to hostile or unwelcoming campus environments that prevent development of positive, meaningful relationships with others on campus or disengage students in classrooms. Theory allows one to "see" in new and different ways that which others might dismiss as old and usual. Theory allows one to feel wonder about topics with which they're quite familiar. I like to say that theory can be used "to exoticize the ordinary" (Besnier, 1995, p. 560) or "to make the ordinary strange" (Jakobson, 1987, p. 25). It can serve as a powerful lens for seeing and therefore understanding our work with college students better.

A Quick Example

A student sitting with a faculty member in the campus café is nothing more than ordinary. But viewed through socialization theory as a lens, this otherwise ordinary encounter is exoticized into social capital exchange. Theory is a way of seeing the world through new introspective eyes.

THEORY AS GLUE

Theory plays many roles in empirical research, one of which is enhancing the rigor of a study by linking together in a logically (or at least, theoretically) connected whole what might otherwise be seen as random, isolated facts. And it's the simple connections across complexities—the glue—that signify rigor (Strayhorn, 2013a). Using theory can help connect hunches, anecdotal evidence, empirical support, to questions, methods, and ultimately conclusions. For instance, my book *Theoretical Frameworks in College Student Research* focused on theory's role in building the argument for a study, focusing the study, developing the research questions, selecting relevant variables, guiding data analysis, and interpreting findings. In short, the book argues theory as the glue that connects different parts of the scientific and writing process. Figure 2.3 provides a summary.

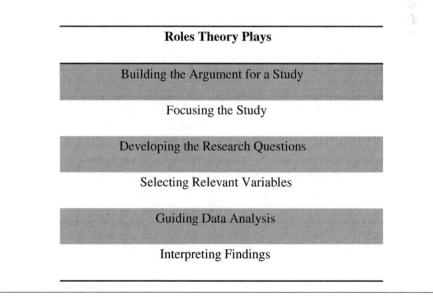

Roles Theory Plays

Building the Argument for a Study

Focusing the Study

Developing the Research Questions

Selecting Relevant Variables

Guiding Data Analysis

Interpreting Findings

Figure 2.3 Framework for using theory in college student research

I tell this story whenever possible (Strayhorn, 2013a). A few years ago, while attending the annual meeting of the Association for the Study of Higher Education (ASHE), I was approached on separate occasions by four doctoral students attending different universities in the United States. Each of them wanted to set a time to talk with me about their dissertation projects—which ranged from the socialization of doctoral students to faculty careers to the institutionalization of academic support programs for Black males. At each conversation it became clear that something was missing, something that grounded the study ("theory as framework"), something that clarified their vision or understanding of the topic ("theory as lens"), something that linked all parts together cohesively ("theory as glue"). What seemed missing was an underlying theory that could be used—like a tool—in conducting the study. As one student proclaimed, "It's the glue that links all of the individual parts together to explain what you're looking at. It helps you design your study" (p. 8). Indeed, it is.

Now that's we've discussed theory as framework, lens, and glue, let's work through a few exercises that require us to apply this new understanding of theory to practice. The next section presents a fictitious reflective exercise, followed by a case study.

QUOTABLE MOMENT

Steven Pinker, a Canadian scientist, said disconnected facts in the mind are like unlinked pages on the web. They might as well not exist.

A MOMENT TO REFLECT

You're Director of Student Activities at Touchstone College. Your immediate supervisor, as Dean of Students, has launched a new initiative that aims to tie the co-curricular involvement activities of Touchstone students to the institution's core learning goal: intellectual development. She asks you to propose at least two activities or programs that hold promise for promoting intellectual development of students at Touchstone College. Additionally, you must explain how the programs you propose relate to college students' intellectual development. It's been a while since your exposure to cognitive development theory in graduate school, but you remember the essence of Perry's intellectual development frame. While you have Perry's intellectual development theory in mind, you're free to use other theories that relate to your objective if you'd like.

A REFLECTIVE EXERCISE

Complete the table below or jot down responses to each part on a seperate sheet of paper.

Proposed Activity	Why It Holds Promise	Relation to Cognitive Development
1.		
2.		
Example:		
Make them take this class	*They'll learn about theory*	*It challenges them to learn new stuff*

A POP QUIZ

Realize it or not, we've already covered a good deal of information about theory, social psychology, and social psychological theories in higher education. For sure there's much more that we will cover in chapters to come. Before proceeding to a case study that provides opportunity for further application, complete this pop quiz.

1. What's positive psychology in your own words?
2. List the "Top Five" student issues you think student affairs professionals deal with on a regular basis, either nationally or on your own campus. Be sure you can defend your choices.
3. With the same professionals in mind from #2 above, how do you think they can use theory in addressing such student issues?
4. Name at least three metaphors of theory.
5. What's the operational definition of theory used in this book?

THEORY TO PRACTICE: A CASE STUDY

A Chinese proverb suggests that example carries more weight than preaching. This wisdom is relevant to our discussion of student development theory in higher education. This case study, like all others included in the book, provides an example to facilitate application of information from the chapter to practice.

Navigate to the Chronicle of Higher Education's website (http://www.chronicle.com). Skim through the list of headlines and find a story involving faculty, staff, or students in which you find interest. Identify the core issue involved in the story. Then complete the following activities with this story or incident in mind.

Case Study Activities

1. Summarize the story or case, including the core issue(s).
2. What role might theory play in helping one understand or "frame" the core issue(s)?
3. What role might theory play in helping one "see" the case in a new and different way?
4. What role might theory play in connecting the story or isolated case to larger, looming issues in higher education?
5. Why do you think the story caught your attention?

CONCLUSION

In some ways, this chapter serves as a primer for those new to the study of social psychological theory in higher education with a strong accent on understanding the role of theory in social science work. It offers an operational definition of theory, several metaphors that have been used in relation to theory, expounds upon three of them, and then moves the more theoretical discussion to practical application for the benefit of all readers. All of this is instructive preparation for what's to come in the chapters ahead. Remember: theory is framework, lens, and glue.

REFLECTIVE EXERCISES

1. Define theory in your own words.
2. List and briefly describe at least three metaphors for theory.
3. What do we mean when we refer to "theory as framework," in this chapter?
4. What do we mean when we refer to "theory as glue," in this chapter?
5. Turn back to the quote from Henry David Thoreau presented in this chapter. How does this quote relate to the principled study of theory in higher education? (Hint: Think about the link between theory as framework and Thoreau's use of "foundation.")
6. Ultimately, what's the goal of theory?
7. Pick two of the following social phenomena and try developing a brief theory for each that plausibly explains the episode: (Encourage students to complete this exercise in groups and share responses)

    a. falling in love
    b. buying a new house
    c. waking abruptly from a bad dream
    d. unfriending someone on Facebook
    e. joining a club in college

CHAPTER SUMMARY

1. Theory is defined as "a set of interrelated constructs, definitions, and propositions that presents a systematic view of phenomena by specifying relations among variables, with the purpose of explaining and predicting phenomena" (Kerlinger, 1986, p. 9).
2. Theory also has been used to refer to plausible explanations of observed phenomena.
3. There are many metaphors that can be used in reference to theory, including conceptual frames, propositions, abstract categories, conceptual maps, stances, and postulations.
4. There are other metaphors for theory such as framework, lens, and glue, each revealing different roles that theory plays in social science.
5. What you see is based, in part, on the lens you use.

DEFINITIONS

Use a dictionary to define the following terms or concepts that relate to the academic study and use of theory.

Chickering's vectors
cognitive dissonance
development
framework
maturation
Perry's positions
theory

RESEARCH TIPS

1. Very few higher education studies, especially theses and dissertations, attempt to generate new theory nowadays. Most opt to use existing theory as a framework, lens, or glue, rather than develop new or different theoretical understandings based on data from a contemporary study. Future researchers are encouraged to see theory development as much-needed and well within their grasp.

2. Tinto (1993) posited an interactionalist theory of college departure that included academic and social integration as pivotal constructs. Yet, Braxton and colleagues (2000) found little to no empirical support for the validity of academic integration in student departure decisions or subsequent commitment to the goal of college completion. Future researchers are encouraged to test the validity of time-honored theories like Tinto's model generally and constructs like academic integration specifically. Studies are needed that determine whether academic integration plays a different role in the process from what was originally envisioned by Tinto.

FURTHER READING

Astin, A.W. (1984). Student involvement: A developmental theory for higher education. *Journal of College Student Personnel, 25,* 297–308.

Becker, H.S. (1993). Theory: The necessary evil. In D.J. Flinders & G.E. Mills (Eds.), *Theory and concepts in qualitative research: Perspectives from the field* (pp. 218–230). New York: Teachers College Press.

Creamer, D.G., & Associates. (1990). *College student development: Theory and practice for the 1990s.* Washington, DC: American College Personnel Association.

Evans, N.J., Forney, D.S., & Guido-DiBrito, F. (1998). *Student development in college: Theory, research, and practice.* San Francisco, CA: Jossey-Bass.

Gardner, H. (1983). *Frames of mind: The theory of multiple intelligences.* New York: Basic.

Jones, S.R., & Abes, E.S. (2011). The nature and uses of theory. In J. Schuh, S.R. Jones, & S.R. Harper (Eds.), *Student services: A handbook for the profession* (5th ed., pp. 149–167). San Francisco, CA: Jossey-Bass.

REFERENCES

Argyris, C., & Schon, D.A. (1974). *Theory in practice: Increasing professional effectiveness.* San Francisco, CA: Jossey-Bass.

Astin, A.W. (1984). Student involvement: A developmental theory for higher education. *Journal of College Student Personnel, 25,* 297–308.

Astin, A.W. (1991). *Assessment for excellence: The philosophy and practice of assessment and evaluation in higher education.* New York: Macmillan.

Ausubel, D.P. (1963). *The psychology of meaningful verbal learning.* New York: Grune and Stratton.

Besnier, N. (1995). The appeal and pitfalls of cross-disciplinary dialogues. In J.A. Russell, J.M. Fernandez-Dols, A.S.R. Manstead, & J.C. Wellenkamp (Eds.), *Everyday conceptions of emotion: An introduction to the psychology, anthropology, and linguistics of emotion* (pp. 559–570). Netherlands: Kluwer Academic Publishers.

Bourdieu, P. (1997). The forms of capital. In A.H. Halsey, H. Lauder, P. Brown, & A.S. Wells (Eds.), *Education: Culture, economy, and society* (pp. 40–58). Oxford: Oxford University Press.

Braxton, J.M., & Lien, L.A. (2000). The viability of academic integration as a central construct in Tinto's interactionalist theory of student departure. In J.M. Braxton (Ed.), *Reworking the student departure puzzle* (pp. 11–28). Nashville, TN: Vanderbilt University Press.

Chickering, A.W. (1969). *Education and identity.* San Francisco, CA: Jossey-Bass.

Coleman, J.S. (1988). Social capital in the creation of human capital. *American Journal of Sociology, 94 Supplement,* 95–120.

Cross, W.E. (1971). Toward a psychology of Black liberation: The Negro-to-black conversion experience. *Black World, 20*(9), 13–27.

Crotty, M. (1998). *The foundation of social research: Meaning and perspective in the research process.* Thousand Oaks, CA: Sage.

D'Augelli, A.R. (1991). Gay men in college: Identity processes and adaptations. *Journal of College Student Development, 32,* 140–146.

Jakobson, R. (1987). On realism in art. In K. Pomorska & S. Rudy (Eds.), *Language in literature* (pp. 25–26). Cambridge, MA: Harvard University Press.

Kerlinger, F.N. (1986). *Foundations of behavioral research* (3rd ed.). New York: Holt, Rinehart, & Winston.

LeCompte, M.D., & Preissle, J. (1993). *Ethnography and qualitative design in educational research* (2nd ed.). San Diego: Academic Press.

Merriam, S.B. (1998). *Qualitative research and case study applications in education.* San Francisco, CA: Jossey-Bass.

Pascarella, E.T., & Terenzini, P.T. (2005). *How college affects students: A third decade of research* (Vol. 2). San Francisco: Jossey-Bass.

Perry, W.G. (1968). *Forms of intellectual and ethical development in the college years: A scheme.* New York: Holt, Rinehart & Winston.

Phinney, J.S. (1990). Ethnic identity in adolescents and adults: Review of research. *Psychological Bulletin, 108,* 499–514.

Strayhorn, T.L. (2006). *Frameworks for assessing learning and development outcomes.* Washington, DC: Council for the Advancement of Standards in Higher Education (CAS).

Strayhorn, T.L. (2008). Influences on labor market outcomes of African American college graduates: A national study. *The Journal of Higher Education, 79*(1), 29–57.

Strayhorn, T.L. (2012). *College students' sense of belonging: A key to educational success.* New York: Routledge.

Strayhorn, T.L. (2013a). *Theoretical frameworks in college student research.* Lanham, MD: University Press of America, Rowman & Littlefield.

Strayhorn, T.L. (Ed.). (2013b). *Living at the intersections: Social identities and Black collegians.* Charlotte, NC: Information Age Publishing.

Tinto, V. (1993). *Leaving college: Rethinking the causes and cures of student attrition* (2nd ed.). Chicago, IL: University of Chicago Press.

Part II

Applications of Theory to Practice

3

ECOLOGICAL SYSTEMS THEORY

An Ethnographic "Glimpse"

Ecological models encompass an evolving body of theory and research concerned with the processes and conditions that govern the lifelong course of human development in the actual environments in which human beings live.

—Urie Bronfenbrenner (1994, p. 1643)

Key Terms

acceptance, alienation, belonging, chronosystem, cohesion, compliance, ecology, exosystem, macrosystem mattering, mesosystem, microsystem, prosocial behaviors, rejection theory

INTRODUCTION

Recall from the first chapter of this book that social psychology is the scientific study of how people think about, influence, and relate to one another. Of course influences on people and their behaviors are not only social psychological in nature. For instance, some are emotional or physiological. Individuals who are sleep-deprived tend to experience more negative emotions, according to studies published in the journal *Social Psychology & Personality Science*. Specifically, Gordon and Chen (2014) found that those who don't sleep well are more likely to experience conflict in their interpersonal relations and they're less able to resolve conflict, regardless of their level of cognitive complexity.

Human behavior is influenced by many factors, including the assumed or real presence of others, one's feelings or emotions, and physiological state. An experimental study conducted at the University of Chicago elicited information from romantic partners about the number of hours spent sleeping, emotional states, and the frequency and nature of interpersonal conflict between the partners over a period of time. Results suggest that physiological states (e.g., sleep deprivation) and other aspects of one's ecology affect individual responses. A take-home message to share with college students and readers of this book—sleep matters!

A MOMENT TO REFLECT

1. What do you know about cognitive complexity and the process through which individuals grow intellectually? List at least one theorist and the core components of their theoretical model.
2. With the theory identified above in mind, list at least two ways you think depressed physiological states such as sleep deprivation compromise one's ability to think complexly.
3. The National Institute of Health advises all individuals to get at least 8 hours of sleep per night. How many hours does the average college student sleep per night, in your opinion? And, how might these sleep patterns relate to the frequency and nature of interpersonal conflicts among roommates, for example?

A major assumption of social psychological models like those featured in this textbook is that context matters. Several recent works emphasize the "call to context" (Delgado, 1995, p. xv). To understand the relationship between individual actors, significant or "instrumental others" (Ceja, 2006) and other factors (e.g., physiological states, emotions) in various contexts or systems, theoretical frames were needed that provided constructs for talking about the relationship between and within such structures. Bronfenbrenner's (1979) *ecological systems theory* is one such frame that posits personal development as a function of reciprocal influences between the individual and the setting(s) that comprise their environment(s) or ecology, a branch of the study of life (i.e., biology) that deals with relations of organisms to one another and their surroundings. Core elements of ecological systems theory are discussed in the next section.

CORE ELEMENTS OF THE THEORY

Bronfenbrenner's (1979) ecological systems theory describes four types of nested systems: microsystem, mesosystem, exosystem, and macrosystem. The microsystem includes all interactions of the individual with their immediate settings (e.g., family, school), while the mesosystem encompasses the interactions of various settings within a given microsystem (e.g., interaction of family and school). The exosystem incorporates institutions in which the individual does not directly participate, but may indirectly influence the individual (e.g., parent's workplace, educational policies). Finally, the macrosystem represents the individual's interactions with cultural norms, beliefs, values, and expectations such as gender socialization or political culture. Each system contains roles, norms, and rules that shape one's development.

Taken together, the four systems represent the nested networks of interactions that reflect an individual's ecology. This ecology changes over time as an individual gets older or as certain systems (e.g., peers, families, schools) become more or less salient to the individual's development; this refers to the chronosystem, which is often described as the fifth system. Chronosystem refers to the collective experiences across an individual's lifetime, including environmental events and major life transitions such as changes in one's family structure through divorce, birth, death or matriculation to college, to name a few. Figure 3.1 presents a graphical depiction of the ecological systems theory.

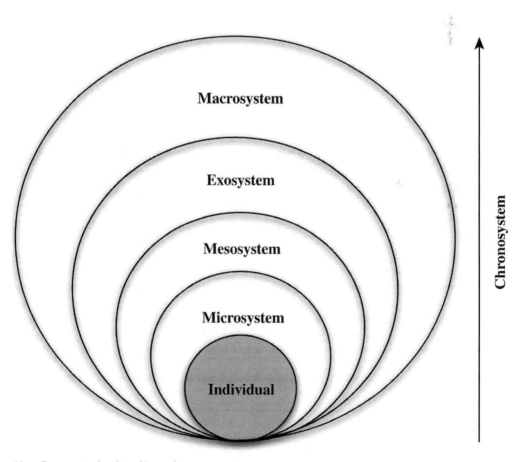

Note. Image was developed by author.

Figure 3.1 Ecological Systems Theory

A POP QUIZ

1. What are the five ecological subsystems that Bronfenbrenner discusses in his model?
2. Think of a particular process of psychological development that relates to college students and try to describe it from the perspective of each of the subsystems included in the model.
3. How does ecological systems theory relate to a college student's racial identity development—that is, the process through which he/she/z assumes a racial identity and comes to understand themselves as such?
4. What information about college student development does an ecological systems approach add to our existing knowledge?

WHAT WE KNOW FROM RESEARCH

A good deal of research has been conducted that sheds light on core elements of Bronfenbrenner's (1979) ecological systems theory or that uses the model as a lens through which to examine a research topic. Several major conclusions flow from prior research that are relevant to this chapter's focus.

First, there is empirical support for the underlying assumption of ecological systems theory—that one's behaviors and experiences are influenced by various spheres of influence. For example, in a previous study, Strayhorn (2010) analyzed data from the National Education Longitudinal Study 1988/2000, sponsored by the U.S. Department of Education, to estimate the net effect of ecological factors on Black high school students' math achievement in grade 10. Results provide persuasive evidence that all three systems affect achievement, accounting for 20% of the variance in student performance. Black students' 10th grade math achievement was significantly associated with locus of control, sex, parental involvement, teacher perceptions, and opportunities to learn. In other words, Black students' who attribute their success to internal factors such as hard work and effort and who benefit from parental involvement in their education tend to score higher than peers on 10th grade math achievement tests.

Second, development is, at first, a consequence of simultaneous interactions between the individual and their immediate environment or microsystem. Microsystem refers to a pattern of activities, roles, and experiences by developing persons in face-to-face settings. And, ecological systems theory suggests that an individual is at the center with increasingly complex spheres of influence around them. Each context or situation provides physical or social features that instigate or inhibit increasingly complex interactions between students and environments (Darling, 2007). For example, Chenoweth and Galliher (2004) studied direct and indirect influences of environment on academic aspirations for rural youth in Appalachia.

A final major conclusion that can be drawn from prior work on ecological systems theory is that there are multiple determinants of development and context matters. Ecological systems theory rejects the common assumptions that developmental attributes (e.g., intelligence, achievement) can be measured or explored out of context of an individual's life, time, and setting. For instance, Renn and Arnold (2003) drew upon

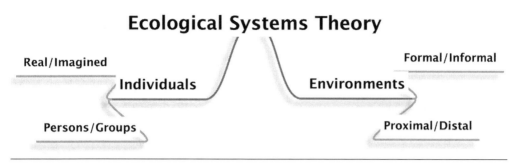

Figure 3.2 Ecological Systems Theory

multiple theoretical frames (e.g., retention, ecological systems) to understand college student peer groups and cultures. They also applied the resulting model to mixed race students, gay students, and honors students enrolled in talent development programs (Linley, 2014; Renn, 2004).

Taken together, previous research studies suggest the utility of ecological systems theory for exploring influences on college student outcomes, learning, and development. The theory directs attention to nested systems, individuals, and groups (real or imagined), and environments (distal or proximal), both those formal and informal. Figure 3.2 presents a graphical depiction of this summary.

THEORY TO PRACTICE: A CASE STUDY

Now that we've discussed ecological systems theory generally, its core concepts, and the ways in which it has been used in prior research (with particular focus on college student studies), an extended example or case study is in order. For this, I draw from my national study of former foster youth who "age out" of the foster care system, yet aspire for or enter higher education (Strayhorn, in press). Although the details of this study require book-length treatment that will likely be my "day job" during a much-needed sabbatical, accept the following points as sufficient background for this discussion:

1. All participants in the study are at least 18 years of age.
2. All participants in the study have "aged out" of the foster care system and, consequently, are expected to possess the skills, abilities, and knowledge necessary for independent, adult living.
3. Over 75% of participants in the study identify as "African American" or "Black," and all are racial/ethnic minorities in higher education.
4. Nearly 65% of participants in the study can be classified as "low-income" since their combined family income or personal income is at or below federal poverty guidelines.
5. Virtually all participants in the study report having been "kicked out" at least once, homeless, verbally harassed or assaulted, or hungry for more than a day.

The purpose of our study of college students formerly in foster care is to understand their academic and social experiences on campus, to highlight their challenges and many successes, and to attempt to build a portrait of who they are, where they enroll, and why they do so. Very little, to date, is known about this special subpopulation of students or what I call "vulnerable population(s)," intentionally challenging the notion that some people are broken or incapable versus vulnerable to poor performance in education due to systems that operate against them. To collect data, my research team and I use semi-structured, one-on-one interviews with willing participants. Interviews are conducted by a trained researcher, while another observes and takes notes about our interactions. All interviews are digitally recorded and subsequently transcribed by a professional.

One of our interview questions asks: "How did you come to choose to go to college?" Responses vary as you might expect, but several converge on similar themes. For example, Keon, an African-American male sophomore majoring in communications, shared the following that reflects the sentiments of a few others:

> I really didn't feel like I had any other choice. I guess other kids do . . . like maybe they feel like they have choices or options, you know. But that's not me . . . that's not my situation or like my reality. I HAD [emphasis added] to go to college. It was college and live or no college and die . . . like that's really how I saw it. [Interviewer: Can you explain or recall why you saw it that way?] Yeah because, for starters, that's what my foster parents told me. They were like, "Ok, Keon, you're getting older now so you got to [sic] stand on your own. So you need to go to college or else you're going to end up paying for it." Then, I just noticed how all my assistance through the system—like insurance, and food card, and other money—just stopped all of a sudden. And my foster parents weren't going to give it to me. Neither were my foster siblings so I just realized that I was going to have to do it myself. And so I came to college, so I can make it somehow.

There are dozens of excerpts like these that line the study's transcripts. What Keon offers is much more than an answer to an interview question. He reveals through his words the ways in which human behaviors are a function of the interaction between a person and his/her/hir environment (Lewin, 1936). He also offers keen insights into the process of personal development as a function of reciprocal influences between the individual and the settings that comprise their ecologies. Keon's decision to attend college was powerfully influenced by multiple levers of social influence. And while true, the same levers may have little to no effect on the college choice decision of another former foster youth in our study. That's the magic of ecological systems theory from a social psychology perspective. It provides constructs for talking about the reciprocal influences between individuals and ecologies. And it affirms that no two individuals are guaranteed to experience social factors, social processes, or interactions the same.

A POP QUIZ

Thinking back to the excerpt from Keon's interview, respond to the following questions to the best of your ability.

1. Identify at least two aspects of Keon's ecology.
2. Sketch an image of Bronfenbrenner's ecological systems theory, using concentric circles as shown in Figure 3.1. Now, list at least one influence or piece of

information about Keon's world on the circle associated with microsystem, mesosystem, exosystem, and macrosystem.

3. Which system of Bronfenbrenner's model represents the influence of foster care policies (e.g., aging out) on Keon's decision to attend college—microsystem, mesosystem, exosystem, or macrosystem?

4. Which system of Bronfenbrenner's model represents the influence of foster parents and siblings on Keon's decision to attend college—microsystem, mesosystem, exosystem, or macrosystem?

5. How does the concept of "chronosystem" relate to Keon's story, in your opinion, if at all?

CONCLUSION

Turning back to the quote that opened this chapter, it's important to remember that "ecological models encompass an evolving body of theory and research concerned with the processes and conditions that govern . . . human development" (Bronfenbrenner, 1994, p. 1643). Information included in this chapter serves as an introduction to those who are interested in learning student development theory from a social psychological approach. Of course, the work of Bronfenbrenner and ecological systems stretches well beyond the confines of higher education research and teaching about student development. By understanding students' contexts, their spheres of influence, their ecologies, we can come to know them better, to forecast their responses, and predict their decisions under certain conditions, at certain times, and with certain currents pushing them in any number of directions.

REFLECTIVE EXERCISES

1. How might students' characteristics and traits predispose them to choose particular peer groups in college?

2. Draw an image or picture that captures the essence of your current understanding about Bronfenbrenner's (1979) ecological systems theory and how ecologies affect college students' experiences and outcomes.

3. Define "ecology" in your own words.

4. What's the difference between "microsystem" and "mesosystem"?

5. Recall the key finding from Gordon and Chen's (2014) research study mentioned in an earlier section of the chapter. What was it? And how might you use this information in your work with students on campus?

CHAPTER SUMMARY

In summary, the purpose of this chapter was to (re)introduce higher education to Bronfenbrenner's (1979) ecological systems theory, as a tool for making sense of college students' experiences and outcomes. Ecological systems theory posits personal development as a function of reciprocal influences between the individual and the settings that comprise one's ecology. Bronfenbrenner's model directs attention to four nested systems and the notion of time: microsystem, mesosystem, exosystem, macrosystem, and chronosystem. Applied to higher education and college student development, ecological systems theory can be useful for understanding the multiple external influences that shape students' social interactions and responses to social stimuli.

DEFINITIONS

chronosystem
ecology
exosystem
macrosystem
mesosystem
microsystem
physiological state
prosocial behaviors

RESEARCH TIPS

1. Ecological systems theory admits dynamism between various spheres of influence that constitute one's ecology. Given that reciprocity, research techniques that accommodate both direct and indirect effects simultaneously are particularly robust for studying ecological systems theory. Structural equation modeling, path analysis, and advanced forms of regression are highly recommended.

2. Ecological systems theory also assumes nested systems, which can be modeled using advanced techniques that permit partitioning variability into multiple levels or hierarchies (e.g., students nested within classrooms, classrooms nested within schools). Hierarchical linear modeling (HLM) is the recommended technique of choice, especially when the variability between levels meets or exceeds 5%. For more about HLM, go to: Raudenbush and Bryk (2002).

3. Studies need not be quantitative. Qualitative methods can be used to explore ecological influences on human behaviors as well. Interview protocols can be fashioned to elicit information about immediate contexts, distal influences, and how these interactions change over time. Probes might include: "which of these most powerfully influenced your decision" or "who did you turn to most often for advice," as mere examples.

4. Education researchers might consider developing new or revising existing datasets to facilitate study of ecological systems and related influences. For instance, higher education scholars might merge institution-level variables from the Integrated Postsecondary Education System (IPEDs) with existing large-scale databases such as the National Survey of Student Engagement (NSSE), College Student Experiences Questionnaire (CSEQ), or Beginning Postsecondary Student Longitudinal Study (BPS).

5. After a close, careful review of existing literature, I found no references to surveys or instruments that measure aspects of ecological systems. Perhaps this is as it should be; perhaps not. Students and postsecondary researchers are encouraged

to think about ways to develop new survey instruments that hold promise for measuring aspects of one's ecology and spheres of influence on social processes, especially in collegiate settings.

FURTHER READING

Bronfenbrenner, U. (1992). Ecological systems theory. In R. Vasta (Ed.), *Six theories of child development: Revised formulations and current issues* (pp. 187–249). London: Jessica Kingsley.

Darling, N. (2007). Ecological systems theory: The person in the center of the circles. *Research in Human Development, 4*(3–4), 203–217.

Galloway, S. (2007). Resilience and ethnic minority college students: Ecological systems perspective. Paper presented at the annual meeting of the Association for the Study of Higher Education, Louisville, Kentucky.

Renn, K.A. (2004). *Mixed race students in college: The ecology of race, identity, and community on campus.* Albany, NY: SUNY Press.

Swartz, J.L., & Martin, W.E., Jr. (1997). Ecological psychology theory: Historical overview and application to educational ecosystems. In J.L. Swartz & W.E. Martin, Jr. (Eds.), *Applied ecological psychology in schools and communities: Assessment and intervention* (pp. 3–27). Hillsdale, NJ: Erlbaum.

REFERENCES

Bronfenbrenner, U. (1979). *The ecology of human development.* Cambridge, MA: Harvard University Press.

Bronfenbrenner, U. (1994). Ecological models of human development. In T. Husen & T.N. Postlethwaite (Eds.), *International encyclopedia of education* (2nd ed., Vol. 3, pp. 1643–1647). Oxford: Pergamon Press.

Bronfenbrenner, U. (1997). Ecological models of human development. In M. Gauvain & M. Cole (Eds.), *Readings on the development of children* (2nd ed., pp. 37–43). New York: W.H. Freeman and Company.

Ceja, M. (2006). Understanding the role of parents and siblings as information sources in the college choice process of Chicana students. *Journal of College Student Development, 47*(1), 87–104.

Chenoweth, E., & Galliher, R.V. (2004). Factors influencing college aspirations of rural West Virginia high schools. *Journal of Research in Rural Education, 19*(2).

Darling, N. (2007). Ecological systems theory: The person in the center of the circles. *Research in Human Development, 4*(3–4), 203–217.

Delgado, R. (1995). *Critical race theory: The cutting edge.* Philadelphia: Temple University Press.

Gordon, A.M., & Chen, S. (2014). The role of sleep in interpersonal conflict: Do sleepless nights mean worse fights? *Social Psychological & Personality Science, 5*(2), 168–175.

Hurtado, S., & Carter, D.F. (1997). Effects of college transition and perceptions of campus racial climate on Latino college students' sense of belonging. *Sociology of Education, 70*(4), 324–345.

Lewin, K. (1936). *Principles of topological psychology.* New York: McGraw-Hill.

Linley, J.L. (2014). *Examining the academic microsystems of successful lesbian, gay, bisexual, and transgender science, technology, engineering, and mathematics majors.* Paper presented at the Annual meeting of the American Educational Research Association, Philadelphia, PA.

Raudenbush, S.W. & Bryk, A.S. (2002). *Hierarchical linear models: Applications and data analysis methods* (2nd ed.). Thousand Oaks, CA: Sage Publications.

Renn, K.A. (2004). *Mixed race students in college: The ecology of race, identity, and community on campus.* Albany, NY: SUNY Press.

Renn, K.A., & Arnold, K.D. (2003). Reconceptualizing research on college student peer culture. *The Journal of Higher Education, 74*(3), 261–291.

Strayhorn, T.L. (2010). The role of schools, families, and psychological variables on math acheivement of Black high school students. *The High School Journal, 93*(4), 177–194.

Strayhorn, T.L. (in press). Finding their way in college or making it: Experiences of former foster youth in higher education. *Journal of College Student Development.*

4

SENSE OF BELONGING IN COLLEGE

A Fresh Perspective

> If psychology has erred with regard to the need to belong . . . the error has not been to deny the existence of such a motive as much as to underappreciate it.
>
> —**Baumeister and Leary (1995, p. 522)**

Key Terms

acceptance, alienation, belonging, cohesion, community, compliance, marginality, mattering, rejection, social affiliation

INTRODUCTION

A couple of years ago, I wrote a book about college students' sense of belonging (Strayhorn, 2012), produced by the same publisher of this textbook. Interestingly, I did not have sense of belonging in mind at all when I set out to write that book. I thought that I was writing a book similar to my *Evolving Challenges of Black College Students*, published by Stylus (Strayhorn & Terrell, 2010). That edited book included chapters from over a dozen authors who shared timeless insights about the contemporary challenges that Black students face in higher education, from striving to excel academically to resolving identity developmental crises. Of course, the new book would differ from the former text in a number of ways. It would be sole-authored versus a collection of edited chapters written by others. It would focus on diverse college students, not just Black students. And I saw it as a data-based book; by that I mean that it would flow from findings that have accumulated over the years in my research studies on college students.

About a week after taking pen to paper (well, finger to computer keyboard . . .), I noticed an undeniable, though unexpected, pattern to my writing. The chapter on Black students ended with a discussion of community, engagement, and belonging. A chapter on Latino students quickly moved from cultural factors like language, heritage, and machismo to extended paragraphs about *comunidades* (community) and

41

sentido de pertenencia (sense of belonging). Turning attention to gay students of color or those majoring in science, technology, engineering, and math (STEM) did not escape the inevitable discussion about community, groups, social affiliation, and how mattering to others seemed to build lasting connections that made belonging possible in college. At some point it was clear to me that sense of belonging was the connective tissue of the book and I made a strong pivot in that direction by retitling the text, reframing each chapter, and embracing rather than resisting the urge to approach topics of community and belonging. It made writing easier and, based on reviews from the field, I think it makes reading enjoyable and a whole lot less redundant.

It has been almost three years since I wrote *College Students' Sense of Belonging: A Key to Educational Success for All Students* and my thoughts about belonging continue to evolve. Some of this is the usual evolution of theoretical insights that one expects when charting new terrain about a subject. Other forces push my views about college students' sense of belonging. For instance, I have had meaningful conversations with educational psychologists like Deleon Gray (North Carolina State University), sociologists like Phil Bowman (University of Michigan), and cultural anthropologists like Amy Shuman (The Ohio State University) who compel me to think about the impact of others' perceptions, social contexts, and cultural artifacts on one's belonging, respectively. In many ways, this chapter is a result of those "moving" conversations. While the main structure of the framework remains virtually unchanged, explanation of the model (i.e., core elements and tenets) in this chapter is a fresh perspective.

Core elements of belonging theory are discussed in the next section.

CORE ELEMENTS OF THE MODEL

As presented in the prior text (Strayhorn, 2012), there are seven core elements of sense of belonging theory.

1. Sense of belonging is a basic human need. Quite simply, all people yearn to belong and find acceptance from others. Belongingness is a universal need and applies to all people. Satisfying the need for belonging is a necessary precondition for higher-order needs such as the desire for knowledge, understanding, and self-actualization (Maslow, 1962).

Evidence? Glad you asked. A few years ago, I traveled to Rome, Italy to deliver a research paper at the European Association of Institutional Research (EAIR) Forum. My first time in Rome, first time in Italy, but I was certainly no newcomer to academic conferences. Confident in my findings from the study, as well as my ability to deliver an interesting, engaging 15-minute presentation with PowerPoint slides as my guide, I felt at home at EAIR, amongst academics, strangers camouflaged by our shared thirst for new information. While the décor of the Forum reminded me of my "academic home," Rome initially evoked an acute nostalgia for anything familiar. I became frustrated with my inability to communicate fluently (having studied Spanish for years, not Italian). Selfishly, I longed for a return to chicken on my flat noodles and coffee over espresso. Most importantly, I wanted to meet someone with whom I could relate personally, talk extensively, and visit the Colosseum. Meaningful interactions of this kind would build social bonds that would help me feel a sense of belonging (in Rome, Italy). Long story short, I met a woman (Tammi) at the downtown train station with whom I connected. We visited a few sights, engaged in extensive conversations, and ultimately built a sense of small, but growing, community. With my few friends and our shared experiences, I started to feel connected, part of, a sense of belonging. Indeed, belonging is a basic human need, universal to all.

2. Sense of belonging is a fundamental motive, sufficient to drive human behavior. Not only is sense of belonging a basic human need, universal to all, but it also acts as a motivation for human behaviors. An appetite to belong "stimulates goal-directed activity designed to satisfy it" (Baumeister & Leary, 1995, p. 500). Individuals are compelled to act to satisfy their need to belong. Recall my story of Tammi in downtown Rome, Italy. I yearned for community and belongingness in Italy's capital city and that basic desire compelled me to jump-start conversation with Tammi when our paths crossed at the train station. Whereas I might have remained silent under other conditions, my need to belong drove me to open up, talk, and initiate conversation with the Italian stranger.

There is no shortage of other examples about how this operates in our daily lives. It's why some people pay to join particular churches, faith groups, fraternities and sororities. It's why some soldiers joined the military, while other would-be soldiers joined the police squad, special services, and politics. And it's why the student you met today in your office showed up in the first place: belonging. Belonging is a basic human need and fundamental motive sufficient to drive human behaviors (Strayhorn, 2012).

Let's not be naïve about it though. The need to belong does not always compel individuals to act in ways that are positive, prosocial, productive, or even democratic for that matter. For example, in their desperation or longing to belong, some impressionable youth "may join a [street] gang or also worship Satan" (Clark, 1992, p. 289). Belonging compels some people to stay in romantic relationships long after "goodbye" was appropriate, even when there are clear signs of danger to their own physical and psychological well-being. Belonging drives some college students who seek social acceptance, affiliation, and membership in Greek-letter organizations to subject themselves to excessive force, sexual assault, and other forms of hazing despite laws that prohibit it. And I have seen gay students deny their sexual identity, Black students reject their cultural interests, and poor students pose as wealthy descendants of fictional royalty all in its name. Indeed, all people want to feel cared about, needed, valued, and part of something connected to others. That basic need to belong will compel them to act in order to achieve the desired goal.

3. Sense of belonging takes on heightened importance (a) *in certain contexts* such as being a newcomer to an otherwise established group, (b) *at certain times* such as [late] adolescence when individuals begin to consider who they are (or wish to be) and (c) *among certain populations*, especially those who are marginalized or inclined to feel alienated in particular contexts (for more Goodenow, 1993a). Sense of belonging is a basic human need and motive sufficient to drive behaviors, but it also takes on heighted importance in specific contexts, times, and populations. The example will soon be overdrawn but here again I direct attention to my story of Tammi, the Italian stranger, who offered me conversation, connectedness, communion, and ultimately belongingness in a context that was *unfamiliar* and at a time when I felt *like an outsider.* Under such conditions, it is typical to retreat, to resist the strange in favor of the known, to cling to that which is common and comfortable. But belonging took on heightened importance for me in Rome — so much so that I once agreed to eat food that I don't enjoy just to spend more time with my few friends versus being alone abroad.

4. Sense of belonging is related to, and seemingly a consequence of, mattering. As I've said elsewhere (Strayhorn, 2012), mattering matters, especially when it comes to belonging. Mattering is defined as feeling, right or wrong, that one matters, is valued or appreciated by others (Schlossberg, 1985). Mattering accents the relational aspect of sense of belonging—the social synergy that creates strong social bonds through the distinctive contributions one makes to the whole.

Rosenberg and McCollough (1981) identified five (5) dimensions of mattering: (a) attention (i.e., noticed in ways that command interest), (b) importance (i.e., object of another's concern), (c) dependence (i.e., feeling needed), (d) appreciated (i.e., feeling respected), and (e) ego extension (i.e., believing others share in your success). Mattering matters. And to feel like they matter, the person must believe someone cares about them.

SENSE OF BELONGING AND MATTERING

Sense of belonging is a basic human need and fundamental motive sufficient to drive human behaviors, even among college students. One's need to belong also shifts with context, time, and space. Belonging is related to mattering and mattering matters, as we've discussed in this chapter.

A BRIEF ACTIVITY

1. Define *mattering*.
2. List at least four synonyms for mattering.
3. Thinking about the important role that mattering plays in facilitating a sense of belonging and ultimately college student success, brainstorm and list at least three ways educators can effectively signal that students matter.

5. Social identities intersect and affect college students' sense of belonging. My conversations with other scholars and some of my most recent work (Strayhorn, 2013b) have extended my initial thoughts about sense of belonging in a number of ways. I still believe it is a basic human need, universal to all, that can motivate human behaviors. While a universal need, it may not necessarily apply to all people equally. Social identities such as race, gender, sexual orientation, and religion converge and intersect in ways that simultaneously influence aspects of one's sense of belonging. For example, take two White college students. One may feel at home on campus, ready to interact with others and establish meaningful relationships that *matter* from the first day of school. The other, however, may struggle to connect with others who are different from themselves or they may choose to join a fraternity, drama club, or sports team as a way of satisfying their need to belong. Similar students, similar needs, but different strategies—this feature of intersectionality is relevant to a discussion of belonging.

To understand students' belonging experiences, one must pay close attention to issues of identity, identity salience, ascendancy of certain needs, and social contexts that exert influence on these considerations. We like to disaggregate students' identities and campus experiences into discernible steps, stages, phases, categories, and time periods that, while useful for empirical research, carry little meaning for students' real-life adaptations. The take-home point is this—social identities intersect and affect sense of belonging. So there can be no silver bullet for building belonging for students and what works for the proverbial "goose" (student A) may not work well or at all for the "gander" (student B).

6. *Sense of belonging engenders other positive outcomes.* The end of all of this is to achieve desired goals, one of which is a feeling of belonging, fitting in, or membership in the group. There are other positive outcomes that flow from finding belonging generally and feeling a sense of belonging in college specifically. For example, belonging has been linked to community service, academic performance, well-being, happiness, and overall health (e.g., Hausmann, Schofield, & Woods, 2007). Belonging is connected to college persistence in a number of ways, including the fact that students who find a sense of belonging on campus do so through strong social affiliations with faculty, staff, and/or students that attach them to the institution—they feel stuck to the campus. Stuck to the institution through the unrelenting adhesion of personal bonds, these students thrive, flourish, and persist in college since quitting or dropping out would require severance of the social ties that bind them to people, clubs and organizations, or departments on campus.

Truth is, most people strive to preserve existing relationships, especially those in which they personally invested (Hazan & Shaver, 1994a, 1994b). Most people feel anxious about the prospect of losing meaningful relationships and thus work to keep them or avoid anxiety. Termination of existing relationships often results in depression, grief, and loneliness (Baumeister & Leary, 1995). Rather than face negative consequences associated with terminating existing relations, "the mass of men [and women] lead lives of quiet desperation," quoting Henry David Thoreau (1971), or come up with justifications for why termination is in their best interest. Still others satisfy their need to belong by devoting the time and energy needed to maintain and preserve previously established relationships.

7. *Sense of belonging must be satisfied on a continual basis and likely changes as circumstances, conditions, and contexts change.* Sense of belonging is a basic human need, universal to all, yet it is anything but static. Just because one feels as if they belong at home does not mean that they will find that sense at work, in school, or on the playing field. Belonging is "largely malleable and susceptible to influence in both positive and negative directions" (Goodenow, 1993b, p. 81).

Several things can disrupt, interrupt, or alter one's sense of belonging in college. For example, changing or transferring schools can disrupt belonging. Disruption can have negative consequences such as isolation, maladjustment, and feeling prone to dropping out of college. To fit back in, individuals must engage again in activities and interactions that foster belongingness all in hopes of regaining a sense of acceptance, mattering, and inclusion. Of course not all activities or experiences that fostered belonging in one context (e.g., institution A) will produce the same effect in another setting (e.g., institution B). Satisfying belonging needs on a continual basis may require different approaches, strategies, and people. Figure 4.1 presents a graphical summary of the theory's core elements.

Given the focus of this textbook, it seems important to connect any discussion of sense of belonging to the larger theme of social psychological theory. What makes sense of belonging appropriate for a textbook on student development theory in higher education from a social psychological perspective? Recall that a social psychological approach directs attention to the influence of the implied, imagined, or actual presence of others on an individual. In this case, a social psychological view of belonging moves from merely understanding *what individuals do* to create or satisfy belonging, which is important, to examining how the presence and actions of others influence sense of belonging for an individual or group.

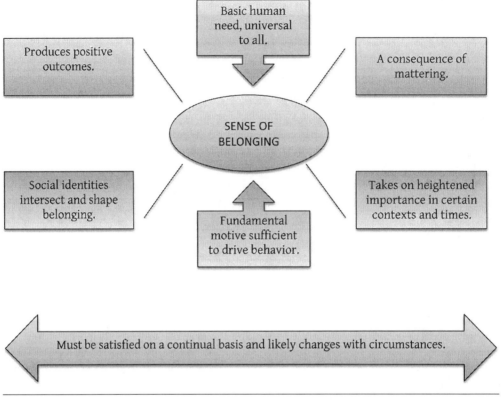

Figure 4.1 Core elements of belonging theory

A POP QUIZ

1. What's social psychology in your own words?
2. What's an operational definition of sense of belonging in college?
3. How might college students find, create, or achieve a sense of belonging on campus?
4. How might the implied, imagined, *and* actual presence of others influence a student's sense of belonging on campus? Be sure to discuss all three forms of presence.

WHAT WE KNOW FROM RESEARCH

A good deal of what we know about college student experiences focuses on what students do and the energy they devote to campus activities (Strayhorn, 2013a). Beyond these topics, prior college student research suggests the importance of warm, welcoming environments that nurture students' sense of belonging on campus and belonging has been posited as a key to educational success for all students (Strayhorn, 2012). Sense of belonging research in higher education has two major thrusts beyond the core elements that were presented in the previous section of this chapter.

First, one line of inquiry focuses closely on conceptual understanding of belonging as a construct in educational contexts (Baumeister & Leary, 1995; Goodenow, 1993a; Ostrove, 2003). Here researchers have worked to distinguish community, *a feeling of fellowship*, from sense of belonging, *perceived fit within a social system*. Definitions of belonging vary from a general sense of social acceptance to "an individual's sense of identification or positioning in relation to a group or to the college community, which may yield an affective response" (Tovar & Simon, 2010, p. 200).

Another category of belonging scholarship explores the role that sense of belonging plays in college students' experiences on campus. Of course some of this work pre-dates the solid focus on "belonging" per se and directs attention to alienation or marginalization, which are states marked by the absence of belonging (e.g., Loo & Rolison, 1986; Suen, 1983). Studies have demonstrated that sense of belonging is positively associated with academic performance, satisfaction with college, and engagement in educationally purposeful activities like clubs and organizations, tutoring, and talking with a faculty member (Hurtado & Carter, 1997; Museus & Maramba, 2011; Strayhorn, 2008a, 2008b).

CAMPUSES AS MICROCOSMS

College campuses tend to be microcosms of the world surrounding them. Forces that shape social relations in the larger society also affect how college students interact with their peers, faculty members, and staff. Social pathologies that pervade communities adjacent to campus or the country at large also mark the collective character of campus.

A BRIEF ACTIVITY

1. Define *microcosm*, using a dictionary online or through a smart device.
2. List at least one issue or social force that shapes social relations in the larger society, state, or community where your institution is located.
3. Describe and explain how the issue you identified in #2 above affects social relations between students, faculty members, and/or staff on your campus.

THEORY TO PRACTICE: A CASE STUDY

Lamont College is a four-year, residential, private liberal arts institution located in Pulaski, Tennessee, the county seat of Giles County. Census data indicate that there were approximately 7,800 people residing in the city as of Census 2000, although the population of Pulaski swells a bit when classes are in session at Lamont College. The median family income was $27,459.

With fewer than 1,000 students on campus, Lamont College boasts offering students a chance to live and learn as part of a small learning community. In fact, the public relations office uses the school's acronym "LC", for Lamont College, in its campaign branding the institution as a **L**earning **C**ommunity.

Campus Co

Without Community, We Per

The word community usually conjures up sentiments of fellowship, sharing, and positive vibes. In fact, most people define community as a group of individuals who share characteristics and goals in common, all working toward a common good. And the same is usually true of campus communities. Well, true until recently.

Over the last few weeks--since the very start of school--the campus has witnessed a number of incidents that do violence to community. Racist remarks spray-painted on historic Hallowed Hall.

Anti-semitic ads hacked into the campus' internet server which displayed on the university's mainpage. A Black-face party, alleged sexual assault during a fraternity hazing incident, and now the immediate termination of a popular academic advisor who happens to be Latino. And we're only in the 4th week of classes....

If we know anything at all, we know that community is vital for cooperation and people co-operate where they belong. But nowadays relatively few students on campus feel as if they belong at

Ren
foll
imp

The
that
rela
the
beh
of a
exp:
in li
its
beh
con
or v

It m
tote
thin
dec
mos
retu

Figure 4.2 Campus news article for "A Case Study"

Though generally quaint and quiet, Lamont College has experienced a rash of negative incidents since the start of classes that do violence to campus community. During the first week of school residents driving through the campus witnessed "riff-raffs in hoodies", as one professor put it, defacing historic Hallowed Hall with spray-painted racist graffiti and offensive epithets. The following week, campus administrators received late-night calls from students complaining about anti-Semitic advertisements that seemed to consume bandwidth and cluttered the university's main page on the Internet. Whatever it was and however it worked, the more people accessed the webpage, the more the virus spread like wildfire. Eventually the university's server crashed and a later investigation revealed that the virus came from hackers off-campus. And as if that was not enough, Lamont's community was negatively affected again by other events such as a black-face party, sexual assault report, hazing, and protests about the unexpected termination of a Latino academic advisor who criticized the institution for "letting diversity numbers decrease to almost nil, while increasing financial support for the all-White male row team." Read the news article shown in Figure 4.2 to gain a sense of how these events have affected campus climate, then answer the questions in the next section using information from the case as a guide.

Case Study Activity

1. Using the Internet, locate information about "Pulaski, Tennessee." What can you learn about the city, its history, and demographic composition? How is this information relevant to or useful for interpreting issues presented in the case? Think back to our ecological systems discussion.
2. Identify at least two of the core issues presented in the case, in your opinion. It may be helpful to establish an operational definition of *core issue* first.
3. In higher education and student affairs, we often encourage students to "assume positive intent" even when there has been negative impact. Personally, I have struggled for years to know how useful this approach is in hostile, offensive, or racist encounters. Let's try it in this activity. Complete the following table, based on information presented in the case or acquired from your Internet search:

INCIDENT	PLAUSIBLE INTENT	LIKELY IMPACT
Defacing Hallowed Hall	Negative: Positive:	
Anti-Semitic online ads	Negative: Positive:	
Black-face party	Negative: Positive:	
Fraternity hazing	Negative: Positive:	
Firing Latino advisor	Negative: Positive:	
EXAMPLE: **"Skipping this activity"**	**Negative: To disengage from the study of social psych theory** **Positive: Excited and can't wait to get to the next chapter of the book**	**Negative: Those who skip this activity will miss an important learning opportunity and rob themselves of deeper understanding of belonging**

4. How useful was "assuming [plausible] intent" in #3 above for analyzing issues in the case? Where was it noticeably difficult to assume positive intent? What might this mean for your work with college students both now and in the future?

5. What is the writer's main thesis in the news story drawn from the September 16 edition of the *Campus Communicator* (see Figure 4.2)?

6. Thinking back to the core tenets of belonging theory, how does each apply to the writer's story and use of the terms community and belonging?

7. Using information from this chapter or your other courses, identify at least two promising strategies for addressing the campus climate issues presented in the case that may foster belonging for students at Lamont College.

REFLECTIVE EXERCISES

1. Define social psychology.
2. Define sense of belonging.
3. What's the difference between sense of belonging and alienation?
4. What's the difference between community and sense of belonging?
5. Name at least one of the core tenets of belonging theory and briefly explain what it means in terms of college student success.
6. In Chapter 9 on "Hope Theory", there is an extended narrative about Tasha (see heading, "A Moment to Reflect"). In her commencement speech, Tasha says, "But over time, I found refuge and relief in good things . . . and the welcoming campus community that we call 'The Earlham Family.'"
   Questions: How are community and belonging related to Tasha's notion of fictive kin or family? In your opinion, what are the pros and cons associated with higher education personnel building family-like environments on campus, or serving as fictive kin, surrogate parents, or family-like members to students? (Remember: Think both pros *and* cons.)

CONCLUSION

College students' sense of belonging is a key to educational success for all students. Simply put, students who feel as if they belong, fit in, matter, and are accepted as members of the campus community excel in higher education. Those who feel as if they do not belong or are alienated from others tend to perform poorly, transfer, drop out, or withdraw altogether. Of course there are important nuances to the belonging story, so to speak. For instance, there is some new evidence arguing that some students may prefer to "stand out" versus fit in (Gray, 2014), although this information awaits empirical testing in higher education fields. And it's also unclear whether students strive to "stand out" as unique, different *individuals* or deploy standing out amongst others as an act of resistance. Answers to these questions and more will only enhance our collective understanding of belonging as a basic human need, a fundamental motive sufficient to drive human behavior, a consequence of mattering, and, yes, key to educational success for all students.

CHAPTER SUMMARY

1. Sense of belonging is a basic human need, universal to all.
2. Sense of belonging is a fundamental motive, sufficient to drive human behavior.

3. Sense of belonging takes on heightened importance in certain contexts, at certain times, and among certain populations.
4. Sense of belonging is related to, and seemingly a consequence of, mattering.
5. Social identities intersect and affect college students' sense of belonging.
6. Sense of belonging engenders other positive outcomes.
7. Sense of belonging must be satisfied on a continual basis and likely changes as circumstances, conditions, and contexts change.
8. College campuses tend to be microcosms of the world surrounding them; forces that shape social relations in the larger society can influence the nature of belonging relationships on campus.
9. Assume positive intent when possible, but admit when there has been negative impact.

DEFINITIONS

acceptance: conformity that involves both acting and behaving in accordance with social pressure

alienation: a withdrawing or separation of a person or a person's affections from an object or position of former (or desired) attachment

belonging: contains both cognitive and affective elements in that the individual's cognitive evaluation of his or her role in relation to the group results in an affective response (Hurtado & Carter, 1997, p. 328)

cohesion: the extent to which a group and its members are bound together, such as by attraction for one another or commitment to each other; a "we" feeling

compliance: conformity that involves publicly acting in accordance with dominant rules, expectations, or standards usually set by others

marginality: the state of being barely within or below a standard of social acceptability; feeling or being located at the edge or periphery of consciousness

mattering: feeling, rightly or wrongly, that one matters, is valued and appreciated by others; consists of five dimensions including attention, importance, dependence, appreciation, and ego extension

rejection: dismissing or refusing a person's affections, proposals, or ideas; denying an individual social acceptability

RESEARCH TIPS

1. Sense of belonging in higher education is a relatively new area of research, although the empirical base is growing steadily.
2. New tools and inventories are needed to measure sense of belonging for college students. Survey items should be developed to assess various core elements such as belonging needs, motives, and aspects of mattering. For instance, some survey items might ask individuals to rate the extent to which they feel accepted, respected, and fairly treated by others on campus. Appropriate analytic methods can be used to determine whether items represent separate, distinct factors and the interrelationships between them.
3. People use the phrase "find a sense of belonging" frequently. Prevalence of this statement in the existing literature on school belonging, community, and higher

education is somewhat ironic since we seem to know very little about *how individuals find* a sense of belonging in education contexts. In fact, most scholars would likely argue that belonging is neither a fixed object awaiting discovery, nor a final destination that students find as they navigate their way through school. Instead, belonging is built, created, facilitated, or nurtured, among other things. Qualitative methods may be useful for unearthing *how this process unfolds*. Future researchers are encouraged to contemplate using case study, ethnography, phenomenology, or grounded theory to advance what we know about belonging in higher education.

4. Almost all that is written about sense of belonging focuses on students. Future studies are needed that explore sense of belonging and its correlates for faculty members, staff, alumni, and recent graduates.

FURTHER READING

Brazzell, J.C. (2001). A sense of belonging. *About Campus, January/February*, 31–32.

Hagerty, B.M.K., Lynch-Bauer, J., Patusky, K., Bouwsema, M., & Collier, P.J. (1992). Sense of belonging: A vital mental health concept. *Archives of Psychiatric Nursing, 6*, 172–177.

Osterman, K.F. (2000). Students' need for belonging in the school community. *Review of Educational Research, 70*(3), 323–367.

Strayhorn, T.L. (2012). *Inalienable rights: Life, liberty and the pursuit of belonging.* Paper presented at the TEDx conference. Retrieved from http://tedxtalks.ted.com/video/Inalienable-Rights-Life-Liberty

REFERENCES

Baumeister, R.F., & Leary, M.R. (1995). The need to belong: Desire for interpersonal attachment as a fundamental human motivation. *Psychological Bulletin, 117*, 497–529.

Clark, C.M. (1992). Deviant adolescent subcultures: Assessment strategies and clinical interventions. *Adolescence, 27*, 283–293.

Goodenow, C. (1993a). Classroom belonging among early adolescent students: Relationships to motivation and achievement. *Journal of Early Adolescence, 13*, 21–43.

Goodenow, C. (1993b). The psychological sense of school membership among adolescents: Scale development and educational correlates. *Psychology in the Schools, 30*, 79–90.

Gray, D.L. (2014). Understanding STEM-focused high school students' perceptions of task importance: The role of "standing out" and "fitting in" in mathematics classes. *Contemporary Educational Psychology, 39*, 29–41.

Hausmann, L.R.M., Schofield, J.W., & Woods, R.L. (2007). Sense of belonging as a predictor of intentions to persist among African American and White first-year college students. *Research in Higher Education, 48*(7), 803–839.

Hazan, C., & Shaver, P.R. (1994a). Attachment as an organizational framework for research on close relationships. *Psychological Inquiry, 5*, 1–22.

Hazan, C., & Shaver, P.R. (1994b). Deeper into attachment theory. *Psychological Inquiry, 5*, 68–79.

Hurtado, S., & Carter, D.F. (1997). Effects of college transition and perceptions of campus racial climate on Latino college students' sense of belonging. *Sociology of Education, 70*(4), 324–345.

Loo, C.M., & Rolison, G. (1986). Alienation of ethnic minority students at a predominantly White university. *Journal of Higher Education, 57*(1), 58–77.

Maslow, A.H. (1962). *Toward a psychology of being.* New York: van Nostrand Reinhold.

Museus, S.D., & Maramba, D.C. (2011). The impact of culture on Filipino American students' sense of belonging. *The Review of Higher Education, 34*(2), 231–258.

Ostrove, J.M. (2003). Belonging and wanting: Meanings of social class background for women's constructions of their college experience. *Journal of Social Issues, 59*, 771–784.

Rosenberg, M., & McCullough, B.C. (1981). Mattering: Inferred significance and mental health among adolescents. *Research in Community Mental Health, 2*, 163–182.

Schlossberg, N.K. (1985). *Marginality and mattering: A life span approach*. Paper presented at the annual meeting of the American Psychological Association, Los Angeles, CA.

Strayhorn, T.L. (2008a). Fittin' in: Do diverse interactions with peers affect sense of belonging for Black men at predominantly White institutions? *The NASPA Journal, 45*(4), 501–527.

Strayhorn, T.L. (2008b). Sentido de pertenencia: A hierarchical analysis predicting sense of belonging among Latino college students. *Journal of Hispanic Higher Education, 7*(4), 301–320.

Strayhorn, T.L. (2012). *College students' sense of belonging: A key to educational success*. New York: Routledge.

Strayhorn, T.L. (2013a). *Theoretical frameworks in college student research*. Lanham, MD: University Press of America, Rowman & Littlefield.

Strayhorn, T.L. (Ed.). (2013b). *Living at the intersections: Social identities and Black collegians*. Charlotte, NC: Information Age Publishing.

Strayhorn, T.L., & Terrell, M.C. (Eds.). (2010). *The evolving challenges of Black college students: New insights for policy, practice, and research*. Sterling, VA: Stylus Publications.

Suen, H.K. (1983). Alienation and attrition of Black college students on a predominantly White campus. *Journal of College Student Personnel*, 117–121.

Thoreau, H.D. (1971). *Walden*. Princeton, NJ: Princeton University Press.

Tovar, E., & Simon, M.A. (2010). Factorial structure and invariance analysis of the sense of belonging scales. *Measurement and Evaluation in Counseling and Development, 43*, 199–217.

5

GROUP CONTACT THEORY

Prejudice and Discrimination

There are few people whom I really love, and still fewer of whom I think well. The more I see of the world, the more am I dissatisfied with it; and every day confirms my belief of the inconsistency of all human characters, and of the little dependence that can be placed on the appearance of merit or sense.

—**Jane Austen,** ***Pride and Prejudice***

Vanity and pride are different things, though the words are often used synonymously. A person may be proud without being vain. Pride relates more to our opinion of ourselves, vanity to what we would have others think of us.

—**Jane Austen,** ***Pride and Prejudice***

Key Terms

bias, discrimination, homophobia, intergroup contact, prejudice, pride, privilege, racism, sexism, status

INTRODUCTION

In 1813, English novelist, Jane Austen, published *Pride and Prejudice*, a romantic fiction centered on Elizabeth Bennet, the story's main character, who overcomes her prejudice toward a wealthy estate owner, Mr. Fitzwilliam Darcy, while he overcomes his pride, compelling the two of them to surrender to their love for each other. A classic love story, Austen's (1813/1988) novel deals with issues of education, morality, manners, and prejudice. It reflects early nineteenth-century England, a society marked by limited social mobility, strong class-consciousness, and systemic stratification. Social divisions were deeply rooted in demographic (e.g., race/ethnicity, gender) and class differences. Personal worth was based, in large part, on external merit (i.e., rank, file, possessions) rather than internal merit (i.e., goodness) and human dignity.

Many readers of this textbook will likely be familiar with Austen's *Pride and Prejudice*, perhaps having read it in high school or undergraduate study. So what does a romantic fiction novel have to do with social psychological theory? The answer is somewhat simple. Elizabeth Bennet's prejudice existed only to the extent that Darcy was present. That's not to say that she did not harbor such feelings, knowingly or unknowingly, when Darcy was not present; in fact, she likely did and visited those prejudices upon individuals who were *like* Darcy. Similarly, Darcy's pride was problematic "in the eye [and presence] of the beholder," again not arguing that Darcy himself could not become frustrated with his own vanity. Both pride and prejudice are social phenomena that are influenced by or understood through the actual, implied, or imagined presence of others. For instance, pride is defined as high or inordinate opinion of one's own dignity, merit, or superiority; the latter term is usually interpreted in comparison with others who would be deemed inferior. This is the link between Austen's novel and the focus of the present chapter.

This chapter focuses on issues of prejudice and discrimination, using intergroup contact theory as a guiding framework. Addressing this topic is important for several reasons. First, prejudice and discrimination are ubiquitous in the United States generally and higher education specifically. For too many years and too many reasons, faculty and staff *pre-judge* students' abilities based on race, class, gender, and other social identities. Students, too, make unconfirmed judgments about faculty members, their teaching styles, and political opinions way before ever encountering them in the classroom. Sometimes these unfavorable opinions are based on little to no first-hand knowledge of the professor's background or approach but rather anecdotes, rumors, or simple lies from the student "grapevine," so to speak. Clearly, prejudices can be seemingly harmless or flattering (e.g., "all gay people are creative") but have serious impact on subsequent beliefs, experiences, and the way in which others perceive individuals. So no matter how harmless it may seem in one setting, prejudice is something that we want to remedy society of everywhere.

There are other reasons why it is important to address this topic. Prejudice and stereotypes often lead to discrimination—that is, unjustly (or illegally) denying individuals access to information, opportunities, or experiences based on the group to which one belongs. Discrimination might also involve unfair or disparate treatment of people based on categorical membership; for instance, U.S. Bureau of Justice statistics suggest that Black males have a 32% chance of going to jail in their lifetime, compared with just 6% for White males. It's not that Black males are disproportionately more likely than White males to commit crimes that will land them in jail, but rather that Black males are often *pre-judged* to be criminals based on *stereotypes* that cast them as thugs, rule-breakers, incorrigible, and threatening. The very presence and awareness of such racist stereotypes influence the psyche of young Black men and correctional authorities such as security guards, cops, lawyers, and judges who come to see Black males as criminals and, thus, treat them like criminals, monitor them like criminals (i.e., surveillance), and lock them up like criminals, a process whereby prejudices lead to discrimination based on stereotypes that become self-fulfilling prophecy.

Finally, discrimination is a problem because it is unjust, unfair, and, in most cases, illegal. But discrimination also is troublesome because it can blemish stellar reputations, mar proud histories, and cost institutions millions of dollars in long court battles. Before presenting the core elements of the theory, let's take a moment to reflect.

A MOMENT TO REFLECT

Two quotes began this chapter on prejudice and discrimination, both of which were drawn from Austen's *Pride and Prejudice*:

> There are few people whom I really love, and still fewer of whom I think well. The more I see of the world, the more am I dissatisfied with it; and every day confirms my belief of the inconsistency of all human characters, and of the little dependence that can be placed on the appearance of merit or sense.
>
> Vanity and pride are different things, though the words are often used synonymously. A person may be proud without being vain. Pride relates more to our opinion of ourselves, vanity to what we would have others think of us.

Quotes can be useful for capturing the essence of various plots and scenes in the novel. With both of these quotes from the book in mind, consider the questions in the next section followed by discussion of the core elements of group contact theory.

A REFLECTIVE EXERCISE

1. The first quote reflects a rather pessimistic outlook—"the more I see of the world, the more am I dissatisfied with it, and every day confirms my belief of the inconsistency of all human characters." Despite its gloomy outlook, I often hear perspectives like this from graduate students and new professionals across the country. The more one experiences of higher education, the more convinced they might become that higher education will not change. *What's your outlook on higher education? How do you feel about the profession and your ability to effect change within it? How can we work together to prevent feeling powerless or pessimistic?*
2. "Vanity and pride are different things." So too are prejudice and discrimination. Use a dictionary, online or through your smartphone, to locate a definition of each term. *Briefly describe how they're different.*
3. If "pride relates more to our opinion of ourselves," then is it reasonable to suggest that prejudice relates to our opinion(s) of others? *YES* or *NO.*
4. Use the following matrix to log, in COLUMN B, your current opinions about individuals or groups listed in COLUMN A and the source of your opinions in COLUMN C:

COLUMN A *GROUPS*	*COLUMN B* *CURRENT OPINIONS*	*COLUMN C* *SOURCE OF OPINIONS*
Policemen		
Teachers		
Elderly		
Prostitutes		
Thugs		
"The Poor"		
EXAMPLE:		
Christians	*holy, single, deep, sober*	*media, Bible, I know some*

CORE ELEMENTS OF THE THEORY

Generally speaking there is no single theory of prejudice or discrimination. Instead, we have fairly extensive information about prejudice, what it is, and what it is based upon. Similarly, we have information that connects prejudice to discrimination, generally through discussion of stereotypes. Given the importance of social interaction as a near-necessary condition for prejudice and discrimination, I judged group contact theory as an appropriate framework for linking these disparate concepts together, offering language for talking about such constructs, and providing theoretical scaffolding for applying them to our work in higher education. This section of the chapter is organized around these three core elements.

What's Prejudice?

Prejudice is *one* concept with *many* definitions. For instance, some define prejudice as "an unfavorable opinion or feeling formed beforehand [in advance] or without knowledge, thought, or reason" (Prejudice, 2011). Despite the diversity of definitions, most scholars agree that it involves negative pre-judgments about individuals or members of a group. Prejudice is pre-conceived and refers to baseless and typically negative attitudes toward another person[s] or members of a group. Common attributes of prejudice include negative feelings or attitudes, stereotyped beliefs, and a tendency or inclination to discriminate against members of the group (Plous, 2003).

Prejudice can be based on myriad factors and social categories that hold significance in society, including age, sex, sexual orientation, religion, socioeconomic status or class, and the social construction called "race" (Bobo & Fox, 2003). Decades of research attention have been directed to common types of prejudice: ageism, sexism, homophobia, religious prejudice, and racism (Herek, 1993; Plous, 2003). Indeed, prejudice is virtually an integral part of human experience.

Scholars have spent many, many years trying to understand the origins of prejudice. For example, Fishbein (2002) argued a genetic basis of prejudice, as well as a cultural evolutionary origin of judgments formed without knowledge or information. Extensive discussion of the genetic heritage of prejudice goes beyond the scope of this textbook, although interested readers are encouraged to read Fishbein's over 300-page volume on the topic.

Culture, however, relates to prejudice in that culture determines the value assigned to various groups at certain times and certain places in a cultural moment. Let's consider an example. Cultural norms of the 1950s would have determined the value assigned to African Americans at that time, which in turn, fueled the prejudicial attitudes toward Blacks that characterized that point in the country's racist history. Contemporary cultural norms that reflect current racial thoughts would determine the value assigned to other groups—for example, gays and lesbians or Middle-Eastern Muslims—which in turn perpetuate prejudicial attitudes toward these groups. In short, culture determines value assigned to various groups; less valued members, then, become targets for prejudice and discrimination. As with other cultural values and norms, prejudice and discrimination have to be learned.

What's Discrimination?

Discrimination is defined as unjust, unfair, or disparate treatment based on categorical membership. Discrimination (*the act*) is usually the consequence of prejudice (*attitudes and perceptions*) based on stereotypes. A stereotype is a simplified assumption about a person or group based on prior assumptions, public or social perceptions, prevailing myths, and, at worst, unfounded hunches, local folktales, or fears. Whatever their origin, stereotypes can *appear* innocuous or generally positive (e.g., women are nurturers) or undeniably negative (e.g., Latinos are lazy, gays are predators). Left unchecked, stereotypes can lead to mass proliferation of erroneous beliefs, but they also result in prejudice (i.e., wrong attitudes or perceptions) and discrimination (i.e., unjust actions). The end of social movements has been to rid the world of prejudice and discrimination, although most agree that our progress has been slow and uneven (Fishbein, 2002).

The act of discrimination begins with attitudes, perceptions, and beliefs. Allport (1954) explained that prejudice and stereotypes arise from normal human thinking processes. To make sense of the world around them, people strive (i.e., Maslow's concept of "need") to sort information into manageable categories. This process of categorization and the categories that come from it serve as the basis for making pre-judgments, positively or negatively. For example, the U.S. Census Bureau estimates that the world population exceeds 7 billion—that's a lot of people, far too many to make sense of individually. To help make sense of the 7 billion, we sort the largest group (i.e., world's population) into smaller, manageable categories through a process of categorization whereby we group together those individuals who share certain characteristics in common and create another category for those who relate to each other but stood independent from others. Consequently, we categorize the world's population into Americans, Canadians, Africans, Indians, men and women, northerners and southerners, students and parents, and so on. The categories that flow from the process serve as the basis for making pre-judgments as we come to perceive individuals based on the general tendencies of the group to which they belong. Though not all Americans are wealthy, this is often assumed *about* Americans when they travel abroad. This is a classic example of prejudice at work. Mistreating an American based on such a prejudicial perception is *discrimination.*

Interestingly, research has shown that when it comes to sorting or organizing information about individuals, people tend to minimize differences between people within groups (i.e., assume within-group homogeneity) while exaggerating differences between groups (i.e., optimal intergroup heterogeneity) (Linville, 1998). Individuals struggle to suspend or dismiss pre-existing beliefs about groups in order to make accurate individual judgments. Experimental social psychology has shown that individuals tend to view members of groups outside their own as more homogenous than members of their own group—what researchers call "out-group homogeneity bias." These are important caveats to keep in mind as we move the conversation from prejudice and discrimination to intergroup contact theory.

What's Intergroup Contact Theory?

Allport (1954) proposed that contact between members of different groups under certain conditions can have positive effects such as working to reduce prejudice, prevent intergroup conflict, eliminate discrimination, and thereby improve social relations. Positive effects of intergroup contact occur when social contact transpires under four facilitative conditions: equal group status, common goals, intergroup cooperation, and authority support.

Prior research supports Allport's (1954) initial intergroup contact hypothesis. For example, peer or cross-group friendships seem to reduce prejudice (Pettigrew, 1998). Indeed, most friends are of equal status, strive to achieve common goals, work together in non-compete environment, and are not forced into contact by laws.

Much research has confirmed that contact reduces prejudice and may prevent discrimination. Positive contact reduces prejudice toward African Americans, gay men, and people living with disabilities (Vonofakou, Hewstone, & Voci, 2007). The idea of intergroup contact also drives policy in the United States. Policies have been formulated to facilitate contact as a way of increasing relations between Blacks and Whites, Protestants and Catholics, criminals and citizens (Dixon, Durrheim, & Tredoux, 2007; Schiappa, Gregg, & Hewes, 2006).

What's Stereotyping?

Stereotyping has a number of consequences, most of which are harmful to individuals, offensive to groups, and devastating to broad democratic and educational goals such as community and belonging (Strayhorn, 2012). For instance, the weight of empirical evidence suggests that stereotypes influence individuals' beliefs about others and determine subsequent behaviors and social interactions. So, people who think "those people [over there]" are poor tend to treat "them" poorly. Social psychologists have advanced this line of understanding by showing that stereotypes can be internalized by individuals for whom a stereotype exists, which ultimately becomes self-fulfilling prophecy. Building

Condition	Explanation
Equal group status	Members in the contact situation are of equal status; hierarchical relations are not present.
Common goals	Members in the contact situation rely on each other to achieve common, shared goals.
Intergroup cooperation	Members in the contact situation work together cooperatively in a non-competitive environment.
Authority support	No social or institutional authorities sanction or force contact; authorities support contact however.

Figure 5.1 Allport's (1954) four conditions for intergroup contact

upon the previous example, "those" who are believed to be poor can become convinced of this belief about themselves, even if it's not true or inconsistent with their own experience; this is what Steele (1997) refers to as "stereotype threat." Once a stereotype is internalized, it determines how an individual behaves. Continuing the previous example, a stereotype exists about poor people and people believe this about individuals in the stereotyped group. The group then internalizing such self-beliefs and starts or continues to act like they're poor even if they have, or acquire, the resources to act differently. It is all becoming a self-fulfilling prophecy so to speak.

Before considering how this information can be applied to higher education problems, let's review the core elements and concepts for this chapter.

A POP QUIZ

1. What's positive psychology in your own words?
2. Name at least three constructs from positive psychology.
3. What is your own personal interpretation of the Jane Austen quotes on the first page of this chapter?
4. Define and briefly distinguish the following: prejudice, stereotypes, and discrimination.
5. Which of the following most closely represents the statement "Attractive people are conceited," based on information from the chapter?

   a. Stereotype
   b. Prejudice
   c. Discrimination

WHAT WE KNOW FROM RESEARCH

Decades of research attention have been directed to common types of prejudice: ageism, sexism, homophobia, religious prejudice, and racism (Herek, 1993; Plous, 2003). For example, Huebner, Rebchook, and Kegeles (2004) analyzed data from 1248 gay and bisexual men (59% White, 29% Latino) in three cities located in the southwestern region of the country. They found that 37% of men reported experiences with verbal harassment, 11% with discrimination, and 5% with physical violence. Encountering such anti-gay experiences was associated with age (i.e., being younger), disclosure of one's sexual orientation (i.e., being out), and HIV status (i.e., being positive). Reports of mistreatment also were associated with lower self-esteem and increased odds of suicidal ideation.

There are other studies that focus on understanding prejudice and discrimination among college student samples. For instance, Cabrera and Nora (1994) examined college students' perceptions and alienation. Though a bit dated, Gougis (1986) explored the role of prejudice on academic performance. Interestingly, van Laar, Levin, Sinclair, and Sidanius (2005) studied roommate contact and ethnic attitudes in campus living spaces.

Furthermore, stereotypes threaten the academic success and well-being of those directly affected by the negative belief. For instance, I analyzed survey data from over 200 high-achieving African American scholarship recipients and found evidence of stereotype threat. Students who expected to encounter racism in college and who felt negatively impacted by a racial stereotype were significantly less likely to earn high grades in college compared with their peers who did not feel that way (Strayhorn, 2009). Taken together, prejudice and discrimination are real and influence human interactions.

LITERATURE IN REVIEW

Now that we have reviewed the existing literature on prejudice and discrimination, consider the following questions and answer them to best of your ability:

1. How would you summarize what we know about prejudice and discrimination?
2. How would you summarize what we know about intergroup contact theory?
3. Were you surprised by any major findings from research related to prejudice and discrimination? If so, what were they and why were you surprised?
4. Describe how prejudice, stereotypes, and discrimination are related in your own words.

THEORY TO PRACTICE: A CASE STUDY

The Vice President of Student Affairs at South Central University (SCU) has invited you to advise the Division on reducing racial and sexual identity prejudice among students, especially after a rash of recent negative events on campus. She's also concerned about this issue after reviewing data from a recent campus climate assessment that indicates 94% of students of color "expect to encounter racism" while at SCU and 80% of gay, lesbian, bisexual, and transgender (GLBT) students described the campus as "hostile and threatening." Sixty-four percent of GLBT students "expect to be discriminated against because of their sexual orientation."

There are other issues that signal the current state of the campus's climate. For instance, the Black Student Association (BSA), GLBT student organization, and campus-wide Student Government Association (SGA) co-sponsored a town hall meeting to discuss common and divergent concerns of their respective constituencies. After moments of civil discourse (for more, see Chapter 8), the event erupted into a name-calling "battle royal" when a gay student accused BSA members of being exclusionary, elitist, and racist for "not opening their doors to other students on campus." Here's an excerpt of what ensued:

GLBT student: "Some groups on campus are exclusionary by nature. Like, I'm not being mean but the BSA is practicing illegal segregation. I mean it's wrong to have an organization that's only for one group of students ... I don't think it's fair that they are not opening their doors to other students on campus."

BSA student: "Wait (laughing) ... wait just one minute. We're open. We're open to anyone who wants to join and pay dues, just like any other group. It's just that y'all [sic] don't want to join because most Whites are too racist to join BSA and most gays are too out and free to feel oppressed."

SGA student: "I think that's a bit broad, buddy ... and there's almost no truth to it. You wouldn't want me to start a White students club and you wouldn't want me to blame all Blacks for being violent and dangerous, right? Or for me to say that all Blacks are late all the time."

GLBT student: (laughing) "That's a good one ... because there's a lot of truth to that."

It was not long before the SGA advisor intervened, asked a closing question, and dismissed the event, disappointed about how the courageous conversation disintegrated into mean-spirited name-calling and unbridled airing of prejudices and stereotypes. Indeed, the Division needs your help.

Case Study Activity

1. Using information from the chapter, explain how prejudice occurs and its relation to discrimination and stereotypes, in your own words.
2. Recall the definition of stereotypes and how they operate. What role, if any, did stereotypes play in the conflict at the town hall meeting?
3. Where do you think stereotypes (e.g., Blacks are late) mentioned in the case study originate?
4. How might an administrator apply intergroup contact theory to the issues involved in this case?
5. Identify at least two ways to reduce, if not eliminate, prejudice at SCU, using information from the case and chapter. In other words, what is your recommended plan of action, including short- and long-term steps?

CONCLUSION

This chapter extends our understanding about the effects that prejudice and stereotypes have on discrimination. While some details are still unresolved, it is clear that prejudice (i.e., attitudes and perceptions) are shaped, in part, by stereotypes, which together can lead to discrimination (i.e., action). Information from this chapter seems particularly important given the rapid increase in the frequency and nature of reported cases of discrimination in higher education. To fully understand the complex mechanisms that shape individuals' attitudes, perceptions, and actions, careful attention must be paid not only to stereotypes but cultural beliefs, norms, and values too.

REFLECTIVE EXERCISES

1. "All gay students wear bright colors." This statement is an example of: (a) prejudice, (b) stereotype, or (c) discrimination.
2. Denying Native American students access to highly selective 4-year private universities would be an example of: (a) prejudice, (b) stereotype, or (c) discrimination.
3. Affirmative action in college admissions is based, in part, on purported instances of: (a) prejudice, (b) stereotype, or (c) discrimination.
4. "All college men of color are athletes." This statement is an example of: (a) prejudice, (b) stereotype, or (c) discrimination.
5. A student comes to your office infuriated. You ask what's wrong. She responds that her biology professor referred to her as "Chelsea" today in class, although her name is Le'Andria. Chelsea is another African American female who is enrolled in another section of the course. Extremely offended by the mix-up, Le'Andria feels like this is clear discrimination. What are your thoughts? And what advice would you offer to Le'Andria that might help resolve her feelings?
6. List and briefly define the four conditions necessary for optimal intergroup contact.

CHAPTER SUMMARY

1. Prejudice is defined as an unfavorable opinion or feeling formed beforehand [in advance] or without knowledge, thought, or reason.
2. Common attributes of prejudice include negative feelings or attitudes, stereotyped beliefs, and a tendency or inclination to discriminate against members of the group.
3. Prejudice can be based on myriad factors and social categories that hold significance in society including age, sex, sexual orientation, religion, socioeconomic status, race/ethnicity, or class.
4. Culture determines value assigned to various groups; less valued members, then, become targets for prejudice and discrimination. As with other cultural values and norms, prejudice and discrimination have to be learned.
5. Discrimination is defined as unjust, unfair, or disparate treatment based on categorical membership. Discrimination (*the act*) is usually the consequence of prejudice (*attitudes and perceptions*) based on stereotypes.
6. A stereotype is a simplified assumption about a person or group based on prior assumptions, public or social perceptions, prevailing myths.
7. Experimental social psychology has shown that individuals tend to view members of groups outside their own as more homogenous than members of their own group—what researchers call out-group homogeneity bias.
8. Four necessary conditions for optimal intergroup contact include: equal group status, common goals, intergroup cooperation, and authority support.

DEFINITIONS

Use a dictionary to define the following terms or concepts that relate to this chapter:

bias
discrimination
homophobia
intergroup contact
prejudice
pride
privilege
racism
sexism
status

RESEARCH TIPS

1. To extend existing lines of inquiry, researchers might study *how* prejudicial attitudes and stereotypes are learned early on. Future work might identify linkages, if any, among prejudice, stereotypes, discrimination, and early socialization experiences.
2. It would be wise to devote considerable time and research attention to developing reliable measures for assessing students' prejudicial attitudes, the prevalence of stereotypes, and the frequency and nature of discrimination on college campuses.

3. Without valid instruments to measure the frequency and nature of prejudice, stereotypes, and discrimination, much of what we know about these topics is based on qualitative studies using interviews or reflective essays. Future researchers might employ various techniques to analyze such data to understand the origins of prejudice, prevalence of stereotypes, and experiences of discrimination. Narrative analysis may also be a fruitful approach that yields valuable insights (for more, see Chapter 9).

FURTHER READING

Fishbein, H. D. (2002). *Peer prejudice and discrimination: The origins of prejudice* (2nd ed.). Mahwah, NJ: Lawrence Erlbaum Associates.

Warburg, P. (2007). *Prejudice and discrimination: A personal journey.* Bloomington, IN: Trafford Publishing.

REFERENCES

Allport, G. W. (1954). *The nature of prejudice.* Cambridge, MA: Addison-Wesley.

Austen, J. (1813/1988). *Pride and prejudice.* New York: Oxford University Press.

Bobo, L., & Fox, C. (2003). Race, racism, and discrimination: Bridging problems, methods, and theory in social psychological research. *Social Psychology Quarterly, 66,* 319–332.

Cabrera, A. F., & Nora, A. (1994). College students' perceptions of prejudice and discrimination and their feelings of alienation: A construct validation approach. *Review of Education, Pedagogy, Cultural Studies, 16*(3–4), 387–409.

Dixon, J., Durrheim, K., & Tredoux, C. (2007). Intergroup contact and attitudes toward the principle and practice of racial equality. *Psychological Science, 18,* 867–872.

Fishbein, H. D. (2002). *Peer prejudice and discrimination: The origins of prejudice* (2nd ed.). Mahwah, NJ: Lawrence Erlbaum Associates.

Gougis, R. A. (1986). The effects of prejudice and stress on the academic performance of Black Americans. In: U. Neisser (Ed.). *The school achievement of minority children: New perspectives* (pp. 145–167). Hillsdale, NJ: Lawrence Erlbaum.

Herek, G. M. (1993). Documenting prejudice against lesbians and gay men: The Yale sexual orientation study. *Journal of Homosexuality, 25*(4), 15–30.

Huebner, D. M., Rebchook, G. M., & Kegeles, S. M. (2004). Experiences of harassment, discrimination, and physical violence among young gay and bisexual men. *American Journal of Public Health, 94*(7), 1200–1203.

Linville, P. W. (1998). The heterogeneity of homogeneity. In J. M. Darley & J. Cooper (Eds.), *Attribution and social interaction: The legacy of Edward E. Jones* (pp. 423–462). Washington, DC: American Psychological Association.

Pettigrew, T. F. (1998). Intergroup contact theory. *Annual Review of Pscyhology, 49,* 65–85.

Plous, S. (Ed.). (2003). *Understanding prejudice and discrimination.* New York: McGraw-Hill.

Prejudice. (2011). In: *Merriam-Webster Dictionary.* http://www.m-w.com

Schiappa, E., Gregg, P. B., & Hewes, D. E. (2006). Can one TV show make a difference? Will & Grace and the parasocial contact hypothesis. *Journal of Homosexuality, 51*(4), 15–37.

Steele, C. M. (1997). A threat in the air: How stereotypes shape intellectual identity and performance. *American Psychologist, 52*(6), 613–629.

Strayhorn, T. L. (2009). The burden of proof: A quantitative study of high-achieving Black collegians. *Journal of African American Studies, 13*(4), 375–387.

Strayhorn, T. L. (2012). *College students' sense of belonging: A key to educational success.* New York: Routledge.

van Laar, C., Levin, S., Sinclair, S., & Sidanius, J. (2005). The effect of university roommate contact on ethnic attitudes and behavior. *Journal of Experimental Social Psychology, 41,* 329–345.

Vonofakou, C., Hewstone, M., & Voci, A. (2007). Contact with outgroup friends as a predictor of meta-attitudinal strength and accessibility of attitudes towards gay men. *Journal of Personality and Social Psychology, 92,* 804–820.

6

GRIT AND HARDINESS

A Social Psychological View of Positivity

Key Terms

control, commitment, challenge, goals, grit, hardiness, perseverance, resilience

A PERSONAL REFLECTION

It's a rainy Monday morning and I just walked into Sugar Academy (a pseudonym), a relatively new KIPP Academy located somewhat centrally in an urban Capitol of a midwestern city. The oversized black-and-white clock on the wall posted outside the main office reads 8:45; I'm 15 minutes early for my meeting with the principal whose actual title—"school master"—seemed a bit antiquated, not to mention reminiscent of a salutation that Southern slave owners demanded of their subordinates under threat of physical abuse and unforgiving whippings. Nevertheless, I was invited to the school that day as a student success consultant and my worries about his professional title would need to await a future meeting. I opened the very heavy, metal door that appeared under the sign reading, "Main Office," and approached a wide-eyed, blonde-haired Black woman who stood at the reception counter.

> Woman: Good morning honey! You're adorable. Glad you could make it to be with us. Just have a seat and Mr. Jacks will be with you shortly.
> Me: Thanks! No worries.
> Woman: May I get you some coffee, water, or anything?
> Me: (smiling) I never turn down an invitation to coffee. Yes, coffee would be great. No cream, just sugar please.

After waiting for what felt like an eternity but was likely more like 10 minutes, the woman returned with a Styrofoam cup filled with black coffee in one hand and two packets of sugar and a red stirrer in the other. "Here you go and I'll check to see when Mr. Jacks will be ready for you." As she disappeared from sight around the ominous corner that seemed to lead to a darkened cavern, rather than someone's office, I glanced around and took notice of several postings. The main office walls were nearly plastered with slogans like "Word Hard" and "Keep On Pushing" and "No Excuses." Apart from being particularly encouraging words for any academically striving student, I recognized these signs as manifestations of the underlying KIPP philosophy that has its roots in positive psychology, character education, and perhaps unknowingly, social psychology. Still, I wondered, as I have many times in the past, what effect, if any, such signs have on students' behaviors, feelings, and thoughts? Do students on the verge of giving up find the resources and strength necessary to "Keep On Pushing" when they come across the sign? And how might one answer this question in a meaningful way that yields reliable or credible information to those who champion student success or those responsible for hanging such signs? Questions of this kind swirled in my mind, uninterrupted, while I sipped the lukewarm, bitter coffee that served as my morning's breakfast.

Just then a young man walked in the office, sporting a handsome navy blazer, white button-up collared shirt, wheat-colored Timberland boots, and khaki slacks sitting slightly lower on his waist than most. His hair seemed freshly-cut, all of his lines (i.e., edge-up) were perfectly framing the front of his face, the back of his neck, and the long sideburns that were clearly his doing. His head glistened from the blazing halogen lamp overhead. A new woman appeared and offered to help him. "Jaymein (pronounced 'Jay-me-yun'), what can I do for you, today?" "Well, I need to sign up for tutoring . . . we have a math test coming up and I'm so stressed and nervous, you know," he requested. "You need tutoring?" she asked with clear sounds of disbelief in her voice. "Now you're too good looking a guy to get low grades, Jaymein." Despite the conversation, she reached under the counter, presented a set of papers, and invited him to complete "two sections" and get his parent's signature. Smiling graciously, Jaymein turned, noticed me, head-nodded, then continued out the heavy, metal door to resume his regularly scheduled activities in school.

After the door closed, I wondered about the beliefs embedded in the woman's statement: Where did that idea come from—that physically attractive people are more intelligent than physically unattractive people? Or that those who access tutoring must be performing poorly or receiving low grades? And do students who are praised as smart, intelligent, or attractive perform better than their peers who are not praised for such qualities? My mental brainstorm—literally a "brain-storm" or cognitive disturbance marked by strong winds of wonder, intense moments of electrifying energy, and a deluge of questions followed by more questions—was interrupted momentarily by a crisis of monumental proportions . . . my coffee cup was empty.

Glancing at my watch, I thought that time had stood still for me to observe the world around me in this exclusive, private academy where well-off parents paid approximately $35,000 per year for their son or daughter to study with the "best and the brightest," in hopes of gaining admission to one of the nation's most prestigious universities. The long-hand of my watch was now at the hour mark and I dismissed this calculation initially, thinking that only 15 very long minutes had passed. However, the digital watch posted on the wall behind the counter glowed fiery red with its LED display: 10:00. Contrary to first belief, I had been waiting for 75 minutes and still there was no sign of the original unnamed, but pleasant, office worker or the school master.

Convinced that I had been forgotten, I reached for my blue messenger bag, yellow umbrella, and stood to dismiss myself before the school bell rang and I was trampled by hundreds of driven academy students who were bent on "winning" a seat in the freshman class of their "top choice" university and had no intentions of letting me stand in the way of their goals, physically or otherwise. "Good morning, Doc! Sorry for the brief delay," came a male voice from behind me. I turned and met a familiar face but the name did not come immediately. Searching through my mental rolodex, I stumbled across it finally and greeted him: "Good morning, Principal Jacks. Thanks for inviting me out to the school." I didn't address his gross understatement that labeled my 80-minute wait as "brief," but I couldn't help to wonder if any of his clocks or watches worked.

We turned the darkened corner and walked into an unexpectedly bright, well-lit office with large windows and whiteboard painted walls where the "school master" etched his personal notes, dribblings, and hieroglyphic-like reminders. Our conversation began almost immediately and we touched on a battery of topics: implicit bias and teachers' perceptions of economically disadvantaged students, racial discrimination and how academy students form coalitions in clubs and organizations, and increasingly popular traits such as grit, optimism, and belonging. Before long, my mind was churning again with many more questions than answers. What's grit and how does it shape students' educational trajectories? Or the time students devote to learning? How do teacher expectations, classroom environments, or parental involvement shape students' behaviors, feelings, self-beliefs, or passion to pursue goals, if at all? And, I wonder if Principal Jacks would mind fetching me another cup of coffee?

WHAT'S THE POINT OF THIS STORY?

Whether it's clear or not, there is a relationship between my questions about the motivational signs on the school's walls, the conversation between the office worker and Jaymein, and many of the issues raised by Principal Jacks. All of them center on how individuals are influenced, positively or negatively, by others, which is the essence of social psychology. My questions also encircle an area of inquiry that addresses how the actual, imagined, or implied presence of others affects the learning and development of students in educational contexts such as high schools, private academies, and American colleges. For instance, Jaymein's anxiety could have been heightened by the office worker's proclamation that "good looking" people don't need tutoring, which would leave him with at least two considerations. If in need of tutoring, then he must *not* be good looking. Or, if he *is* good looking, then he would be left to prepare for the test on his own without tutoring. What motivated Jaymein to pursue tutoring anyway? Why didn't he interpret his difficulty in math (perhaps received through "feedback" such as a low grade on a quiz or assignment) as a fixed problem, a sign that he can't succeed, or just cause for changing his goal and enrolling in a lower-level math? Indeed, there are both internal and external dimensions of social psychological factors that help explain how Jaymein remained committed to the goal of turning his alleged low math performance to math success; these are the focus of the present chapter.

There are other questions that I've considered, sometimes while working out in the gym, sitting in the nail shop waiting for a pedicure, or driving down North High Street in Columbus as I make my way from home to campus. For instance, why is my running time so much shorter when I'm running beside my gym buddy versus running alone, although I'm covering the exact same distance? Why are people—mostly White women—so surprised and intrigued (judging by the amount of time spent staring) by my presence in the nail shop, although I'm there to tame my feet and toes just as they are? And why do some people come to complete halts at every stop sign without the threatening presence of police cars, while some drivers place themselves and others at risk by ignoring virtually all rules of road, especially the one that prohibits individuals from "driving at a glacial pace in front of professors when they're rushing to campus for a meeting?" Ok, the latter hypothetical may be a bit too specific, informed by my own experience at a large, public research university located in the Midwest region of the country. Still, all of the phenomena alluded to above or implied by my questions reflect concerns of social psychology.

Questions about the nature of human interactions and how the implied, imagined, or actual presence of others shapes those encounters are likely to be the intellectual curiosities of anyone who counts themselves to be a "people watcher." But people watching, as an informal exercise, is not equivalent to the scientific study of social psychology and its application to the field of higher education and student affairs, which is the focus of this text. A social psychological approach to college student development requires use of multidisciplinary theories, an expansive empirical base, and close attention to the presence and influence of others on individuals. Before moving to a fuller discussion of grit, hardiness, and related concepts, let's do a quick refresh of our working definition of social psychology since you're now over half way through the book.

A REFRESHER ON OUR WORKING DEFINITION OF SOCIAL PSYCHOLOGY

Quite often before scholars can mine an idea for its empirical worth, it is necessary to attend to basic definitions and concerns. For the purposes of this book, social psychology is framed as a concerted, scientific effort "to understand and explain how the thoughts, feelings, and behaviors of individuals are influenced by the actual, imagined, or implied presence of other human beings" (Allport, 1985, p. 10). It is an interdisciplinary field of study that draws upon insights from multiple perspectives (e.g., sociology, psychology, anthropology) to gain a better—more complete—understanding of the individual and how one fits into the larger social system (Alter, Aronson, Darley, Rodriquez, & Ruble, 2010).

This text draws upon a multidisciplinary literature base, by definition, to promote students' understanding of college student development and application of social psychological theory to the principled practice of higher education administration. Social psychology employs scientific methods to explain social behavior. Generally speaking, social psychology centers on the empirical study of social phenomena such as group behavior, social perceptions, conformity, aggression, and prejudice, to name a few.

Social psychology marks itself off from other subfields, such as personality psychology and sociology, in several ways. Personality psychology focuses on individual traits, characteristics, and thoughts that relate to individual expressions or behaviors such as introversion, extraversion, aggressiveness, to name a few. Social psychology directs attention to situations and the influence of aggregate, collective, or group forces on attitudes and behaviors (Digman, 1997). Sociology, on the other hand, emphasizes the role of macro-level institutions and cultures on behavior, including expressly how such institutions operate, how they are constructed and maintained, and how they are situated in larger structures of power and privilege. Social psychologists, however, are more interested in the impact of the social environment and group interactions on attitudes, behaviors, and other observed social phenomena (Allport, 1985). For fuller discussion of this topic, see Chapters 1 and 2 of this volume.

Given the importance of both social contexts, environments, and settings, as well as psychological traits, characteristics, and processes to the aim of social psychology, I draw upon literature from psychology (i.e., personality, cognitive, behavioral), sociology (i.e., social stratification, social class, criminology/deviance), anthropology, education, and related social sciences to frame chapters or issues broached within this book. And while examples are designed to facilitate students' application of material to problems and situations that arise in higher education and student affairs, the core content and theory section of each chapter locates the topic in the relevant disciplinary literature (i.e., using language and citations appropriate for such fields). Chapter information also situates our present-day use of the concept in higher education between the seminal pieces about a topic and more recent studies from the field, and synthesizes information from multiple sources in ways that make explicit reference[s] to the disciplinary connections throughout the text.

WHAT IS POSITIVE PSYCHOLOGY?

As a subfield or near-cousin of psychology, social psychology suffers from some of the same shortcomings for which traditional psychology has been criticized. A virtually exclusive focus on pathology (i.e., what's wrong) has dominated much of psychology, which leads to a model of human life and interactions that are lacking, deficit-filled, and, frankly, not worth living. Such a science, no matter how rigorous, empirical, or "evidence-based," is by necessity incomplete. Contrary to the weight of empirical psychological evidence, life *is* worth living and individuals can be *positively* influenced by the actual, imagined, or implied presence of others. For instance, when one's belonging needs are satisfied by positive, supportive, affirming relationships with friends, personal well-being and social development are optimized (Strayhorn, 2012). Turning attention from the negative consequences of social alienation, rejection, and determinants of low self-esteem to acceptance, belonging, happiness, and well-being is the approach of positive psychology.

Positive psychology is composed of a focus on positive subjective experiences such as optimism or satisfaction, positive individual traits (e.g., love, courage, perseverance), and factors that enable or allow individuals and societies to flourish; the latter focuses on civic virtues that propel collectives such as altruism, civility, and responsibility (Seligman, 2004, 2012). Positive psychology represents a seismic paradigmatic shift from pathology—what's wrong and how to repair damaged human functioning—to building positive qualities and talents in individuals and communities. Rather than a separate subfield, positive psychology might be understood as a particular perspective or mindset within psychology, even social psychology, that casts a critical gaze on identifying and nurturing the genius or strongest qualities in people (and collectives) rather than striving to fix what's wrong with them.

HOW DOES POSITIVE PSYCHOLOGY RELATE
TO SOCIAL PSYCHOLOGY?

It should be clear to readers how positive psychology relates to social psychology (what one might call positive *social* psychology), but let me offer a few points of connection in an attempt to be instructive. First, positive social psychology attempts to explain how the *positive* thoughts, behaviors, traits, and responses of individuals are influenced by the real, imagined, or implied presence of others. Positive psychology just has an explicit focus on positive traits, talents, strengths, and genius. A positive social psychological approach to understanding college students' grit, for instance, might pay close attention to the ways in which the presence of individuals such as mentors or advisors influence students' perseverance toward achieving short- and long-term goals with passion. Building on the personal reflection that opened this chapter, a positive social psychological approach might explore how the wall signs and messaging (e.g., "Just Do It") shapes students' hardiness levels.

Positive psychology, too, leads to theorizing about measurable, observable social phenomena or individual, noncognitive traits such as grit. For instance, Duckworth et al. (2011) offered more than an operational definition of "grit" in her research on military cadets, students, and spelling bee finalists, although that alone is a worthy assignment. She also theorized what grit is, where it comes from, how it can be developed (if at all), and how individuals activate it under stressful circumstances such as national spelling competitions. So what results is more than a positive psychology concept that can be operationalized as a research construct, but a theory of grit that can be employed to understand individuals and how they fit within (and negotiate) their social environment; this is part of a social psychological approach. (We'll return to this point in the next section.)

Lastly, positive psychology is multidisciplinary. Positive psychologists and the theories they advance depend on historical notions, key concepts, and knowledge gained from sociology, psychology, anthropology, and biology, to name a few. From sociologists, positive psychologists gain a perspective on how environments might condition traits such as grit, hardiness, and conscientiousness. Like their psychology peers, positive psychologists direct attention to thoughts and attitudinal patterns. And along with biologists and some health professionals, positive psychologists study the world of the mind, physiological aspects of development, cognitive science, and temporal development of frontal lobes and so on.

Consider the example in the next section that illustrates several connections between positive psychology and social psychology in educational settings.

A QUICK CASE STUDY

A student named Cameron (African American male, standing 6' 2" tall with bright, light-brown eyes and broad shoulders) is sitting in the student union studying for a Chemistry 101 midterm. He's stressed about the test since it covers everything discussed in class and chapter readings since the first day. He's anxious, his palms are sweaty, and he can't focus on the material any longer than 30 minutes. Then, his boyfriend, Jon, walks up behind him, hugs him, and rests his chin on Cameron's shoulder. Jon says: "It's going to be fine, Cam; relax. I know you're going to do well. You got this." All of a sudden, Cameron is happy, relaxed, smiling, and feeling a bit more confident.

Shortly after the two embrace, the Director of the Multicultural Center approaches, greets them with a broad smile, and asks Cameron, "Are you ready for that chemistry test, Cameron?" He replies with a weak smile: "Yes, I'm hopeful . . . if nothing else, I know that I can pull a B. Earlier I was worried but I'm feeling much better about it now."

1. It appears that Cameron went from being anxious and nervous to calm, confident, and happy all in a single sitting. What enabled his happiness? And what role, if any, did Jon play in this?
2. What's the relationship between happiness and well-being? How do they relate to one's interpretation of life events?
3. Cameron tells the multicultural director that he is hopeful about his performance on the test. What's hope? From where does it come? What's its impact on performance? We'll return to this in Chapter 9.
4. What's the difference between hope and optimism? Are they learned or inherited? And when do they begin to distort one's reality, if at all?
5. Using information from the case study, how might we inspire hope and optimism in the students with whom we work?

These are just a few questions that point to the relation between positive psychology and social psychology, especially in the context of higher education and student affairs.

> People don't change that much. Don't waste time trying to put in what was left out. Try to draw out what was left in. That is hard enough.
> —Buckingham and Coffman (1999, p. 57)

WHY A CHAPTER ON POSITIVE PSYCHOLOGY?

So, why include a chapter on positive psychology and related concepts? Good question. I have at least three justifications. First, like positive psychologists, I believe that college student educators are in the business of not only understanding what is but also what could be. By "what is," I mean students in their present state, as they are upon arrival. By "what could be," I'm referring to talent development, growth, or the impact of college on students. Positive psychology provides information that holds promise for promoting college student development.

Second, positive psychology is strengths-based and so much of what we do in higher education today is informed by deficit-based approaches; anti-deficit perspectives are needed. A clear example of an anti-deficit view is the growing use of *StrengthsQuest* in college activities, campus leadership retreats, and even admissions interviews. *StrengthsQuest*, like some other inventories, elicits information from individuals using an online survey. For instance, respondents might choose between a pair of words or phrases like "go with the flow" or "meticulously planned." Responses are scored and participants receive a report that organizes their results into five major strengths themes. A full report also offers recommendations about how the individual can deploy their measured strengths to achieve academic, career, and personal success. Rather than focus on fixing what's wrong or broken, *StrengthsQuest* and other inventories rooted in positive psychology focus on identifying what's right and working and strengthening use of it to maximize success.

Lastly, a good deal of recent scholarship has been devoted to positive psychology and the field, though in its infancy, shows no sign of abating. In my opinion, any contemporary treatment of the topic of student development theory in higher education is incomplete without coverage of positive psychology. Positive psychology theories add to what we currently know about students' psychosocial, cognitive, ethnic identity, and moral development. Theories can also be integrated or combined in use in ways that allow us to see more than any one single theory alone.

One final point about our discussion of positive psychology in a theory textbook focused on a social psychological approach to college student development. Traditional psychologists tend to view college and students' experiences within college from a "what's wrong and needs fixing" perspective; this we've called *negative* psychology. We've known for years that college is a challenging period of life, filled with stressful events. First-year and transfer students face difficulty transitioning from prior communities (e.g., home, high school) to campus and many report serious social adjustment issues including homesickness, alienation, and withdrawal. Even those who transition smoothly or adjust successfully may face academic challenges such as test anxiety, academic probation, stereotype threat, and poor grades. Ethnic and sexual minorities in higher education may face an additional set of stresses including harassment, racism, homophobia, and myriad other social pathologies (Strayhorn & Terrell, 2010). Traditional psychologists have contributed much to our understanding of out-group[ing] processes, racial microaggressions (which I like to say can feel like macroaggressions), and distress, to name a few.

Positive psychologists have identified several protective factors that individuals use to negotiate, reduce, remove or otherwise "work through" life [dis]stresses; three will be discussed in this chapter: grit, hardiness, and resilience. Grit is defined as sustained interest and persistent efforts in passionate pursuit of long-term goals. Related to the courage found in hardiness, grit involves unchanging pursuit of specific goals despite failure and adversity (Duckworth, Peterson, Matthews, & Kelly, 2007). Hardiness, on the other hand, is a pattern of attitudes that helps turn stressful circumstances from potential disasters into growth opportunities (Maddi et al., 2013, p. 128). Hardiness has been referred to as the existential courage to do the hard work that's necessary for changing stress into opulent opportunities for development. Resilience is a less stable, malleable noncognitive trait that can be conditioned and has been shown to be responsive to intervention (Banyard & Cantor, 2004); generally, it is referred to as the capacity to bounce back from setbacks.

A SHORT (BUT POSITIVE) ASSESSMENT

Complete the following exercise using information from the chapter or elsewhere.

1. If you know your five major strengths from *StrengthsQuest*, then list them here. If you don't, consider taking *StrengthsQuest* online and then supplying this information.
2. Complete the following statements to the best of your ability:
   a. The best thing about me is . . .
   b. What I enjoy most about my job is . . .
   c. My most fulfilling experience working with a student was . . .
   d. What I bring to most teams is . . .

WHAT WE'VE LEARNED ABOUT GRIT FROM RESEARCH

Well, before I go too far down this path, I think the first thing to know is that we haven't learned a whole lot yet given the relative youth of this area of research. The few studies that have been done suggest several possible conclusions. These are highlighted below, along with caveats about the perceived generalizability of findings.

Grit research has focused on at least three areas of inquiry. First, scholars have devoted time to initial development and testing of psychometric scales that measure individuals' grit, defined as perseverance and passion for long-term goals (Duckworth et al., 2007). See Figure 6.1 for more about this area of scholarship.

HOW DO YOU SPELL SUCCESS? G-R-I-T

In 2011, Angela Duckworth, a professor in psychology at the University of Pennsylvania, joined with her colleagues to conduct a longitudinal study to understand how children improve in academic skills. Specifically, they used the expert performance framework to test the effectiveness of three preparation strategies (i.e., deliberate practice, reading for pleasure, and quizzing by others) on students' spelling skill. They found that deliberate practice strongly predicted success in the national spelling bee and grit was associated with persistence with deliberate practice activities over other types of preparation. While the correlational design of the study limits causal claims, results lend support to the idea that deliberate practice produces more gritty students or, alternatively, gritty students are inclined toward deliberate practice over other "less gritty" options.

Figure 6.1 Grit research synopsis

A POP QUIZ

Locate a copy of Duckworth et al.'s (2011) study, published in *Social Psychological and Personality Science*. Read the entire article, taking note of how they introduce positive psychology frames, the expert framework, hypotheses, and findings related to grit. Then, respond to the following questions on your own or in groups of no more than four.

1. How do the authors define grit?
2. What are the three preparation strategies outlined in the expert framework?
3. List at least one of the key findings from this study related to grit and deliberate practice. What does it mean in your own words? (For help, see list of "hypotheses" on page 175 of the article.)
4. Based on results from this study and related research, rate the extent to which you agree with the following statements using a scale ranging from 1 (not at all true) to 5 (very much true):

   a. Grittier students are more likely to engage in tutoring, which explains their superior performance.
   b. Grittier students are more likely to be involved on campus, which explains their successful adjustment to college.
   c. Grittier students are more likely to devote time to studying, even when "rushing" to join a fraternity/sorority, which explains their ability to maintain high grades throughout membership intake.

A second area of scholarship has focused on theoretical mining of the concept (grit) to clarify its meaning and its distinction from other personality traits and constructs such as resilience. Grit is much more than mere work; it entails strenuous work in challenging domains, maintaining interest and effort in a task, activity, or goal over long periods of time—even years—despite failure, setback, or "plateaus in progress" (Duckworth et al., 2007, p. 1088). While theoretically related to hardiness (Maddi et al., 2013) and resilience (Brooks & Goldstein, 2002), grit encompasses a bit more about the individual's capacity to stay the course while others would change paths or surrender altogether.

Lastly, grit research, to date, has attempted to test the predictive validity of grit and related concepts for specific samples. Grit has been associated with happiness, life satisfaction, retention in a military training program, and grades at an ivy league college (Duckworth et al., 2011; Duckworth et al., 2007; Duckworth & Quinn, 2009; Roberts, Walton, & Viechtbauer, 2006; Singh & Jha, 2008). For instance, Duckworth and Quinn (2009) analyzed data from 1,248 cadets at West Point, the US Military Academy, and found that grit predicted completion of the academy's rigorous summer training program better than the Whole Candidate Index, composed of one's weighted high school rank, SAT score, involvement, and physical exercise evaluation, which is used for admission. They concluded, "grittier West Point cadets were less likely to drop out during their first summer of training" (p. 173). Similar conclusions have been drawn for National Spelling Bee participants (Duckworth et al., 2011) and public school students in grades 4 through 8 (Rojas, Reser, Usher, & Toland, 2012).

Higher education scholars also have explored grit and its relation to student success. In a survey study of 140 Black males attending predominantly White institutions, Strayhorn (2010) tested the predictive validity of grit in explaining one's undergraduate grade point average (GPA). Grit was positively related to grades for Black males, indicating that grittier Black males earned better grades in college than their less gritty Black male counterparts. Grit and other facts in the model accounted for nearly one-quarter of the variance in college grades for Black males at PWIs. Grit, alone, added incremental predictive validity over and beyond traditional predictors of academic success such as high school GPA and ACT test score.

Grit, as a psychological concept, is situated among work on stable individual traits such as intelligence and IQ (Galton, 1892) and less stable noncognitive traits such as self-confidence, emotional IQ, and resilience (Brooks & Goldstein, 2002). Social psychologists posit that one quality shared by most successful people is grit. It is defined as "perseverance and passion for long-term goals" (Duckworth et al., 2007, p. 1087). Grit involves working strenuously, up-stream in pursuit of one's short- and long-term goals with deliberate passion, despite adversity, failures, and even unanticipated setbacks.

In this exercise, we need a preliminary assessment of your level of grit; we'll use items adapted from Duckworth's (2007) short grit survey that is available in the public domain. Rate the extent to which you agree with the following statements using a 5-point scale ranging from 1 (strongly disagree) to 5 (strongly agree):

1. I finish whatever I begin.
2. My interests never change, hardly ever.

3. I am never discouraged by setbacks.
4. I have no problem focusing on projects or tasks that take a long time to complete.

Now add together your rating for each statement and use the following guide to interpret your score:

SCORE RANGE	INTERPRETATION
16–20	High in grit
11–15	Moderate in grit
6–10	Low in grit
4–5	Very low in grit/unclassified

DIRECTIONS: With your score and interpretation in mind, respond to the following questions on your own or in groups of no more than four.

1. Thinking back, how well does your score and interpretation match what you know about yourself? Specifically, how does it reflect how you manage pursuit of short- and long-term goals over time and circumstance? Share your responses with the group.
2. Can you recall a time when you performed in a way that contradicts your score on the grit scale in the previous section? In other words, if you scored high in grit, then can you recall a time when you abandoned a long-term goal rather quickly without much effort? Or vice versa? Share this with your colleagues. (It's important to remember that there's existing debate about whether grit is a fixed trait or one that changes over time and context.)
3. How might you use information in this section of the chapter in your work with students you engage regularly? Share ideas with your colleagues or develop a list, if you're working alone.

WHAT WE'VE LEARNED ABOUT HARDINESS FROM RESEARCH

As I mentioned earlier, hardiness has been conceptualized as "a pattern of [three] attitudes that helps turn stressful circumstances from potential disasters into growth opportunities" (Maddi et al., 2013, p. 128). It has come to be known as the existential courage that's useful in increasing performance and health despite stress. The pattern of three attitudes (known as the "3 C's") includes commitment, control, and challenge. Commitment reflects the attitude that no matter how hard things get, its best to stay connected or committed to people and events around you, thereby avoiding alienation. Control reflects the attitude that no matter how bad things get, you want to continue to influence outcomes, thereby avoiding powerlessness. Challenge reflects the attitude that no matter how tough things get, stressful circumstances are normal aspects of life and provide opportunities for growth and development through what's learned by dealing with them. Remember—grit is the determination or perseverance to stay the course without changing goals or directions over time and circumstance; hardiness is the courage to learn from what's happening and changing if advantageous or developmentally productive.

Hardiness makes a contribution to positive psychology by expanding it to include courage along with happiness. It is related to persistence, vitality, resilience, although hardiness implies courageous perseverance under stress (Maddi, 2006). And there's increasing evidence that strengths-based personality factors such as hardiness play a key role in determining performance in certain contexts; this is especially true in contexts that are highly stressful, challenging, or threatening to one's well-being such as college.

> Hardiness is known as existential courage. Prior research suggests the effectiveness of hardiness in determining human performance in stressful, challenging, threatening contexts such as traumatic life experiences or even classrooms, test settings, and college campuses.
>
> **QUESTIONS**: How do college campuses pose a threat to students' physical or psychological well-being? How might this impair or delay student development in specific domains? What role, if any, might hardiness play in ensuring college students' success despite stressful campus conditions?

Theorizing about hardiness asserts that this characteristic leads to learning from one's efforts of recognizing and resolving the ongoing stressful circumstances of one's life . . . and growing in wisdom and fulfillment from that process (Maddi et al., 2013, p. 128). Alternatively, people low in hardiness tend to deny or avoid stress, which compromises growth. A substantial empirical base supports this theory of hardiness. For example, hardiness has been associated with enhanced performance, drug use, positive emotionality, religiosity, achievement in college, and other outcomes of psychological functioning (e.g., Maddi, 1999; Maddi, Brow, Khoshaba, & Vaitkus, 2006).

Like grit, hardiness has been operationalized as a form of courage or motivation that helps one deal with stressful circumstances. Both of these have been shown to facilitate resilience under stress (Maddi et al., 2013). Whereas a "gritty" person approaches achievement (and life) as a long marathon that requires stamina, sustained interest, and persistent effort toward unwavering pursuit of short- and long-term goals; the "hardy" individual approaches achievement (and life) as a long run that requires openness to variety and changes as opportunities to grow through what they learn along the way. New paths may become apparent, different strides and pace can lead to growth. No matter what, hardy individuals maintain a high sense of commitment, control, and challenge; to them, life is inherently stressful, full of anticipated, inevitable stressors (e.g., traffic on the highway to work) and unexpected stressors (e.g., downsizing of a company) that must be interpreted, managed, and overcome.

> "Hardy" individuals approach achievement (and life) as a long run that requires openness to variety and changes as chances to develop from what they learn. Hardy individuals maintain high sense of the 3 C's (commitment, control, challenge) despite stress.

APPLICATION TO PRACTICE: HARDINESS TRAINING

Hardiness is a "pattern of attitudes that helps turn stressful circumstances from potential disasters into growth opportunities" (Maddi et al., 2013, p. 128). It has come to be known as the existential courage that's useful in increasing performance and health despite stress. The combination of hardiness attitudes (known as the "3 C's") includes: commitment, control, and challenge.

To get a rough, preliminary assessment of your level of hardiness, rate the extent to which you agree with the following statements using a 5-point scale ranging from 1 (strongly disagree) to 5 (strongly agree):

1. I usually wake up excited to continue or finish up whatever I left unfinished yesterday.
2. I am certain that I can make my plans work out.
3. I generally see change as an opportunity to learn/grow.
4. When I try hard, my efforts accomplish much.

Now add together your rating for each statement and use the following guide to interpret your score:

SCORE RANGE	INTERPRETATION
16–20	High in hardiness
11–15	Moderate in hardiness
6–10	Low in hardiness
4–5	Very low in hardiness/unclassified

DIRECTIONS: With your score and interpretation in mind, respond to the following questions on your own or in groups of no more than four.

1. Thinking back, how well does your score and interpretation match what you know about yourself? Specifically, how does it reflect how you respond to stressful situations? Share your responses with the group.
2. Can you recall a time when you performed in a way that contradicts your score on the example hardiness scale above? In other words, if you scored high in hardiness, then can you recall a time when you behaved as if you were low in hardiness by failing to maintain challenge, commitment, and/or control? Or vice versa? Share this with your colleagues. (It's important to remember that there's existing debate about whether hardiness is a fixed trait or one that changes over time and context.)
3. How might you use information about hardiness in your work with students you engage regularly? Share ideas with your colleagues or develop a list if working alone.

WHAT WE'VE LEARNED ABOUT RESILIENCE FROM RESEARCH

Like so many concepts in social psychology and theory, prior research on resiliency has been conducted to develop a deeper understanding of the concept and to discern how it differs from related concepts like self-efficacy, motivation, and even grit and hardiness (e.g., Maddi, 2004). Resiliency is the ability to bounce back successfully despite growing up in adverse circumstances (Gordon, Padilla, Ford, & Thoresen, 1994). Others explain that resilience is "success in schools [or other settings] despite personal vulnerabilities, adversities brought about by early and ongoing environmental conditions and experiences" (Wang & Gordon, 1994, p. 38). And one of the more succinct definitions suggests that resilience is achievement when achievement is rare for those facing similar circumstances (Gayles, 2005).

Beyond mere definitions, prior research has contributed much to our understanding of factors that fuel one's resiliency. For instance, the weight of evidence consistently links goals, self-beliefs, and mastery experiences to resiliency. Gordon Rouse (2001) analyzed survey data from 64 urban high school sophomores to compare self-concept and motivational patterns among students who were academically resilient or non-resilient, as well as advantaged achievers. She found that resilient students not only outperformed their non-resilient counterparts but goals, environmental support beliefs, cognitive ability beliefs or mindsets conditioned students' resiliency. Similar results were found for hope and self-efficacy (Brooks, 2005).

Other resilience research underscores a number of factors, both biological and psychological, that are associated with resilience. For instance, studies have shown that resilient adolescents are autonomous (Gordon Rouse, 1995), more socially responsible (Garmezy, 1993), and have an internal locus of control (Gordon Rouse, 1995). Additionally, resilient students are purported to be friendly, with superior social skills, and independent (Crosnoe, 2005; Luthar, Cicchetti, & Becker, 2000). One study found that increasing perceived self-efficacy seems to be one of the main processes leading to resilience among adolescents (Harvey & Delfabbro, 2004).

A good deal of research has uncovered social dimensions of resilience and the ways in which social and environmental factors foster resilience in individuals. For example, family factors have been linked to resiliency; family factors include supportive affective ties to family, positive expectations of the child, democratic or open parenting style, and meaningful connections with others who share family-like bonds but are unrelated by birth or biological genetics; like others, I refer to these as "fictive kin" (Gordon Rouse, 2001). Environmental factors range from ties with prosocial adults to attending an institution or college that offers support for recovering from setbacks, overcoming obstacles, or campuses marked by an ethos of high expectations, student success, and recovering successfully from failure (Cicchetti & Toth, 1997).

CONCLUSION

What has been attempted here is a worthy treatment of positive social psychology by way of grit, hardiness, and resilience. The development of these concepts over the last few decades has been traced. This treatment was intended to be comprehensive, not encyclopedic, but also without duplication of information found in other chapters or sections of the book.

Turning back to the personal reflection that began this chapter, I offer the same set of questions as a springboard for the exercises to come in the next section. Those questions are: (a) Where did the idea come from that physically attractive people are more intelligent than physically unattractive people? (b) Or the idea that those who access tutoring must be performing poorly or receiving low grades? (c) Or the idea that students who are praised as smart, intelligent, or attractive perform better than their peers who are not praised for such qualities? And (d) Why Jaymein believed he could improve his performance through tutoring, practice, or mastery experiences? Hopefully this chapter has provided useful insights into these issues.

REFLECTIVE EXERCISES

1. Define positive psychology, in your own words.
2. Define positive *social* psychology, in your own words.
3. Define grit, in your own words.
4. Define hardiness, in your own words.
5. List and briefly define the 3 C's or patterns of attitudes that comprise hardiness.
6. Define resilience, in your own words.
7. Distinguish grit and hardiness from one another using your own words and an example relevant to higher education and student affairs.
8. Distinguish grit *and* hardiness from resiliency using your own words and an example relevant to higher education and student affairs.
9. What's your main take-away(s) from this chapter?

CHAPTER SUMMARY

1. Grit is defined as sustained interest and persistent effort in the passionate pursuit of long-term goals. Related to the courage found in hardiness, grit involves unchanging pursuit of specific goals despite failure and adversity.
2. Hardiness is a pattern of attitudes that helps turn stressful circumstances from potential disaster into growth opportunities. It is the existential courage that is useful for enhancing performance and health despite stress. Hardiness has been conceptualized as the combination of control, commitment, and challenge.
3. Resilience is the ability to bounce back successfully despite growing up in adverse circumstances.
4. Positive psychology focuses on positive subjective experiences, positive individual traits, and factors that enable individuals and societies to flourish and thrive. It casts a critical gaze on identifying and nurturing the strongest qualities in people, not fixing what's wrong with them.

TERMS

Challenge
Commitment
Control
Effort
Grit
Hardiness
Motivation
Perseverance
Positive psychology
Resilience

RESEARCH TIPS

1. Much more research is needed to understand the role that positive psychological constructs such as grit, hardiness, and resilience (even hope and optimism) play in higher education generally and college student success specifically.

2. All three of the concepts introduced in this chapter deserve additional empirical testing in terms of their latent structure, reliability, and validity across various samples. For instance, grit is defined as perseverance with passion toward short- and long-term goals, especially over long(er) periods of time. Existing survey items elicit information about the extent to which individuals consistently complete whatever has begun. Additional survey items can be developed and tested to assess other dimensions of grit, hardiness, and/or resilience. Appropriate analytic methods can be used to determine the underlying structure of hypothesized measures and the interrelationships between survey items and discrete factors.

3. A good deal of research on resiliency includes qualitative studies that explore "how" and "why" students from vulnerable circumstances activate their resiliency to find success in educational contexts, although academic success is rare for similarly situated individuals. Little to no published qualitative research exists on grit and hardiness; future researchers should address this gap by using qualitative methods (e.g., interviews, observations, documents) to advance grit and hardiness lines of inquiry.

FURTHER READING

Seligman, M.E.P. (1990). *Learned optimism*. New York: Alfred A. Knopf.

Tough, P. (2012). *How children succeed: Grit, curiosity, and the hidden power of character*. New York: Houghton Mifflin.

REFERENCES

Allport, G.W. (1985). The historical background of social psychology. In G. Lindzey & E. Aronson (Eds.), *Handbook of social psychology* (Vol. 1, pp. 1–46). New York: Random House.

Alter, A.L., Aronson, J., Darley, J.M., Rodriquez, C., & Ruble, D.N. (2010). Rising to the threat: Reducing stereotype threat by reframing the threat as a challenge. *Journal of Experimental Social Psychology, 46*(1), 166–171.

Banyard, V.L., & Cantor, E.N. (2004). Adjustment to college among trauma survivors: An exploratory study of resilience. *Journal of College Student Development, 45*(2), 207–221.

Brooks, R., & Goldstein, S. (2002). *Nurturing resilience in our children*. Lincolnwood, IL: NTC Publishing Group.

Brooks, R.B. (2005). The power of parenting. In R.B. Brooks & S. Goldstein (Eds.), *Handbook of resilience in children* (pp. 297–314). New York: Kluwer Academic/Plenum.

Buckingham, M., & Coffman, C. (1999). *First, break all the rules: What the world's greatest managers do differently*. New York: Simon & Schuster.

Cicchetti, D., & Toth, S.L. (1997). Transactional ecological systems in developmental psychopathology. In S.S. Luthar, J.A. Burack, D. Cicchetti, & J.R. Weisz (Eds.), *Developmental psychopathology, perspectives on adjustment, risk, and disorder* (pp. 317–349). New York: Cambridge University Press.

Crosnoe, R. (2005). Double disadvantage or signs of resilience? The elementary school contexts of children from Mexican immigrant families. *American Educational Research Journal, 42*(2), 269–303.

Digman, J. (1997). Higher order factors of the Big Five. *Journal of Personality and Social Psychology, 73*, 1246–1256.

Duckworth, A.L., Kirby, T.A., Tsukayama, E., Berstein, H., & Ericsson, K.A. (2011). Deliberate practice spells success: Why grittier competitors triumph at the National Spelling Bee. *Social Psychological and Personality Science, 2*(2), 174–181.

Duckworth, A.L., Peterson, C., Matthews, M.D., & Kelly, D.R. (2007). Grit: Perseverance and passion for long-term goals. *Journal of Personality and Social Psychology, 92*(6), 1087–1101.

Duckworth, A.L., & Quinn, P.D. (2009). Development and validation of the short grit scale (Grit-S). *Journal of Personality Assessment, 91*(2), 166–174.

Galton, F. (1892). *Hereditary genius: An inquiry into its laws and consequences.* London: Macmillan.

Garmezy, N. (1993). Children in poverty: Resilience despite risk. *Psychiatry, 56,* 127–136.

Gayles, J. (2005). Playing the game and paying the price: Academic resilience among three high-achieving African American males. *Anthropology & Education Quarterly, 36*(3), 250–264.

Gordon, K.A., Padilla, A.M., Ford, M.E., & Thoresen, C. (1994). *Resilient students' beliefs about their schooling environment: A possible role in developing goals and motivation.* Paper presented at the annual meeting of the American Educational Research Association, New Orleans, LA.

Gordon Rouse, K.A. (1995). Self-concept and motivational patterns of resilient African American high school students. *Journal of Black Psychology, 21*(3), 239–255.

Gordon Rouse, K.A. (2001). Resilient students' goals and motivation. *Journal of Adolescence, 24*(4), 461–472.

Harvey, J., & Delfabbro, H. (2004). Psychological resilience in disadvantaged youth: A critical overview. *Australian Psychologist, 39,* 3–13.

Luthar, S.S., Cicchetti, D., & Becker, B. (2000). The construct of resilience: A critical evaluation and guidelines for future work. *Child Development, 71,* 543–562.

Maddi, S.R. (1999). The personality construct of hardiness: Effect on experiencing, coping, and strain. *Consulting Psychology Journal, 51,* 83–94.

Maddi, S.R. (2004). The role of hardiness and religiosity in depression and anger. *International Journal of Existential Psychology & Psychotherapy, 1*(1), 38–49.

Maddi, S.R. (2006). Hardiness: The courage to grow from stresses. *The Journal of Positive Psychology, 1*(3), 160–168.

Maddi, S.R., Brow, M., Khoshaba, D.M., & Vaitkus, M. (2006). The relationship of hardiness and religiosity in depression and anger. *Consulting Psychology Journal, 58,* 148–161.

Maddi, S.R., Erwin, L.M., Carmody, C.L., Villarreal, B.J., White, M., & Gundersen, K.K. (2013). Relationship of hardiness, grit, and emotional intelligence to internet addiction, excessive consumer spending, and gambling. *The Journal of Positive Psychology, 8,* 128–134.

Roberts, B.W., Walton, K.E., & Viechtbauer, W. (2006). Patterns of mean-level change in personality traits across the life course: A meta-analysis of longitudinal studies. *Psychological Bulletin, 132,* 1–25.

Rojas, J.P., Reser, J.A., Usher, E.L., & Toland, M.D. (2012). *Psychometric properties of the academic grit scale.* Lexington, KY: University of Kentucky.

Seligman, M.E.P. (2004). *Authentic happiness: Using the new positive psychology to realize your potential for lasting fulfillment.* New York: Atria Books.

Seligman, M.E.P. (2012). *Flourish: A visionary new understanding of happiness and well-being.* New York: Atria Books.

Singh, K., & Jha, S.D. (2008). Positive and negative affect, and grit as predictors of happiness and life satisfaction. *Journal of the Indian Academy of Applied Psychology, 34,* 40–45.

Strayhorn, T.L. (2010). Buoyant believers: Resilience, self-efficacy, and academic success of low-income African American collegians. In T.L. Strayhorn & M.C. Terrell (Eds.), *The evolving challenges of black college students: new insights for policy, practice, and research* (pp. 49–65). Sterling: Stylus Publishing.

Strayhorn, T.L. (2012). *College students' sense of belonging: A key to educational success.* New York: Routledge.

Strayhorn, T.L., & Terrell, M.C. (Eds.). (2010). *The evolving challenges of Black college students: New insights for policy, practice, and research.* Sterling, VA: Stylus.

Wang, M.C., & Gordon, E.W. (1994). *Educational resilience in inner-city America: Challenges and prospects.* Hillsdale, NJ: Lawrence Erlbaum Associates.

7

PERSONALITY THEORY

Three Little Pigs and Big-Five Traits

The ultimate measure of a man is not where he stands in moments of comfort and convenience, but where he stands at times of challenge and controversy.

—Rev. Dr. Martin Luther King, Jr.

Key Terms

agreeableness, character, conscientiousness, extraversion, introversion, neuroticism, personality

INTRODUCTION

Questions about personality are pervasive in higher education, student affairs, and the larger society. Consider this fictitious conversation between two faculty members regarding "Geeta," an Indian female student on campus:

Dr. A: "Geeta is very polite and I enjoy having her in class."
Dr. B: "I agree. In my class, she's punctual, her assignments are well organized and on-time, and I think she's always happy (laughing)."
Dr. A: "That's right. She's such a 'people person,' you know. It's clear that she was brought up well."
Dr. B: "I couldn't agree more. Geeta will be very successful in life."

Conversations of this kind are plentiful in higher education. College student personnel make judgments or assessments of students' potential based on behaviors observed in the classroom, in their office, or on the playing field. It is clear from the script above that the two professors have generally positive things to say about Geeta—she's courteous, punctual, well-prepared for class, and organized. What may be less clear is that the two professors are talking about *the visible aspect of one's inner self, essence, character, especially as perceived by others* (Personality, 2003), which social psychologists refer to as personality. This is the focus of the present chapter.

It's a cliché to say but, in terms of personality, actions speak louder than words. In fact, it has been noted that personality and character are revealed in action not words (Allport, 1985). Think back to the conversation between the two professors; notice how they make conclusions about the student's personality (i.e., her essential character) as polite and well-organized based on the way she treats people in class and the structure and quality of her assignments. It's not that the student *said* that she was polite, courteous, and happy but rather that her *actions* provided sufficient evidence to support their assessments of her character. This is an example of how one's personality is revealed through actions.

Interestingly, there are optimal directions to our evaluation of personality. For example, it is difficult to assess one's own personality but impossible to overlook others. Think about it: look at the person seated next to you (or if you're reading in isolation, think about a person with whom you recently interacted) and jot down a few notes about their personality. What words come to mind? What's good about them? What's less-than-good or annoying? Now think about yourself. What are your personality strengths? And what are your weaknesses? I rest my case. You see, it's far more difficult to assess one's own personality but nearly impossible to overlook others, no matter how good or less-than-good.

A MOMENT TO REFLECT

This chapter opened with a quote from Rev. Dr. Martin Luther King, Jr., still regarded as one of the world's most influential civil rights activists. Born January 15, 1929 as Michael King to a family of southern Baptist preachers, young Michael, later Martin, was known to be a bit of a risktaker. In fact, it is fairly well known that Martin was attending a public parade, against his parents' wishes, when news broke that his grandmother had died. He was a hardworking student and voracious reader at Booker T. Washington High School and skipped two grades. He enrolled in Morehouse College at age 15. Despite his father's conservative religious views, Martin drank beer, played billiards, and partied in college. In seminary, he was deeply impressed by the works and thoughts of Reinhold Niebuhr whose theology of Christian realism resonated with Martin's growing beliefs in nonviolent civil protest.

Martin preached fiery sermons about freedom, justice, and human rights. He often talked about how easy it is to be angry and violent, acting out one's deep frustrations with the delay of justice by fighting, killing, or looting. A consistent opponent of violence, Dr. King advocated a higher commitment to nonviolent social change. In his opinion, nonviolent direct action took courage, control, and power. These underlying beliefs led him to say: "The ultimate measure of a man is not where he stands in moments of comfort and convenience, but where he stands at times of challenge and controversy."

A REFLECTIVE EXERCISE

1. Why do you think Michael King, Sr. (the civil rights activist's father) changed his name to Martin Luther King, Sr. and what might this reveal about his personality? [Hint: A simple web search on your smartphone will yield lots of information.]

2. Historians often characterize young Martin as a risktaker. What evidence does the story above provide to substantiate or challenge their claims?
3. Given all that you know about Rev. Dr. Martin Luther King, Jr., to date, how would you characterize his personality? Write down the words you would use to do so.
4. Do you agree with the statement that personality and character are revealed in actions not words? TRUE or FALSE

Core elements of personality theory are discussed in the next section.

Think back to when you were a kid and the fable of the "Three Little Pigs." What do you remember about them? Recall that one built a house made of straw, another of wood, and another of bricks. The big bad wolf was able to huff, puff, and blow down the houses made of straw and wood; the one made of brick, a more durable substance, withstood the pressure. How does this relate to personality, in your opinion?

CORE ELEMENTS OF THE THEORY

Personality theory, per se, does not exist. There is no single theory about personality that guides our collective understanding of what personality is, how it develops, and how it affects social interactions and phenomena. It is possible, however, to synthesize what we know to outline the broad brushstrokes of what might be viewed as a theory or *plausible explanation* about personality. This is outlined below.

First, what is personality? Personality is generally defined as a visible aspect of one's inner self, essence, or character, especially as perceived by others. It refers to a person's collection of qualities. In other words, some believe that a single quality or trait is just that—a quality or trait; personality, on the other hand, is what results from the constellation of qualities and traits that are peculiar to a person or distinguishes one from another. Think of it this way—personality is the sum total of the physical, mental, emotional, social character of an individual (McCrae & Costa, 1997; Personality, 2003). See Figure 7.1 for a visual depiction of these points.

Our operational definition of personality is helpful for discussing how personality relates to behavior and social contexts; remember, social psychology directs attention to the influence of the implied, imagined, or actual presence of others on one's personality or distinctive character. Here, scholars have long since agreed with Gordon Allport's view of personality (Allport, 1954). Allport is often regarded as the founder of humanistic psychology. Unlike Sigmund Freud and other famous psychologists, Allport did not have a medical or clinical background and thus approached questions of being and personality from a different vantage point. He argued that animals are different from humans, kids are different from adults, and antisocial, abnormal or neurotic behaviors

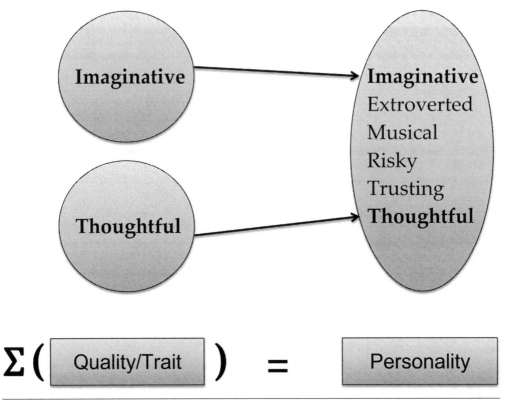

Figure 7.1 Qualities, traits, and personality

are *qualitatively* different from prosocial, normal, or healthy ones and these distinct dif-ferences must be considered when theorizing.

Three major themes that emanate from Allport's (1985) work are the consistency of personality, social influence, and concepts of self or "ego." Although it may vary over time and space, it is generally agreed upon that personality is stable and certainly becomes more and more stable as one matures. It also is true that personality is influ-enced socially. There are individual and common traits and the latter are those charac-teristics that many people share such as emotional stability and adaptability.

Another perspective that drives our understanding of personality is Kurt Lewin's (1951) theory that human behavior is a function of the person and the environment. His theory is represented by this equation: $B = f (P \times E)$, read as "human behavior is a function of the person times (or interacting) with the environment." Not only do individuals react to their environment, but they also shape their environment (and are shaped by it); it is a reciprocally dynamic process. The interaction of the person (dimen-sions of personality) and environment (situation) determines the behavior (outcome). For instance, heat can interact with butter and cause it to melt. That same heat can interact with an egg and cause it to cook. Applied to higher education, one student can interact with a group of individuals, establish meaningful social connections and persist. Another student with a distinct personality can interact with the *same group* of individuals, find it difficult to establish relationships, and drop out of college altogether. Indeed, B = f (P × E).

> Personality is that which permits a prediction of what a person will do in a given situation.
>
> —R. B. Cattell (1950, p. 2)

A POP QUIZ

1. What's positive psychology in your own words?
2. Name at least three constructs from positive psychology.
3. What is your own personal interpretation of the quote from Dr. Martin Luther King, Jr. on the first page of this chapter?
4. Define personality in your own words.
5. List the three themes drawn from Gordon Allport's work.
6. Kurt Lewin's theory of human behavior is represented as ___ = f (___ × ___).

WHAT WE KNOW FROM RESEARCH

Apart from theoretical explanations about personality and traits, we know a good deal from empirical research about personality and its associative properties. One line of research distinguishes traits (i.e., a basic dimension of personality) from personalities (i.e., collection of distinctive qualities) and offers various taxonomies for such qualities (Allport, 1985; Lewin, 1951). Revisit Figure 7.1 that provides a visual illustration of this distinction.

A separate line of inquiry focuses on measurement of personality. A significant literature supports a five-factor model that accounts for data patterns (McCrae & Costa, 1997). Specifically, the Big-Five personality traits include: extraversion, agreeableness, openness, conscientiousness, and neuroticism. For example, the five-factor model posits extraversion as the opposite of introversion, neuroticism as the opposite of emotional stability. Figure 7.2 presents a summary of the Big-Five personality traits.

For years, researchers have been invested in personality and its measurement (Allport, 1954; Barrick & Mount, 1991; Lewin, 1936). Personality can be measured using rating or Likert-type scales. For instance, the Big-Five personality traits can be assessed using an inventory that asks individuals to rate the extent to which they see themselves as talkative, inventive, moody, considerate, and reliable, to name a few (John & Srivastava, 1999). Individual item scores range from 1 ("disagree strongly") to 5 ("agree strongly") and the 44-item inventory can be scored along each dimension of the Big-Five factors.

There are other popular instruments that purport to measure aspects of one's personality. For example, it's probably true that every reader of this book has taken the Myers-Briggs Type Indicator (MBTI) assessment. The MBTI was developed by and named after Isabel Briggs Myers and, her mother, Katharine Briggs, who created the instrument as a

Big-Five Trait	Examples
Extraversion	Emotional expression, excitability, energetic
Agreeableness	Trust, affection, civility
Openness	Imagination, creativity
Conscientiousness	Thoughtfulness, impulse control
Neuroticism	Emotional stability, anxiety, moody

Figure 7.2 Big-Five personality traits

Source: Five traits based on McCrae & Costa, 1997

way of making type theory accessible to the masses. Based on the psychological theory work of Carl Jung (1971) who argued that what appears to be random behaviors are, in fact, systematic differences in the ways that people deploy their mental capacities, especially in terms of perceptions and judgments. Perception refers to one's awareness of things, people, and events, while judgment refers to the conclusions that one draws from such perceptions.

The MBTI is based on several important questions about a person. Consider the following:

1. Where does one prefer to direct attention? Outward world (*extraversion*) or inward to inner world (*introversion*).
2. How does one prefer to receive information? As received (*sensing*) or through interpretation or meaningmaking (*intuition*).
3. How does one make decisions based on such information? Logic (*thinking*) or sensibilities (*feelings*).
4. In dealing with the world, does one prefer to make decisions and deadlines (*judging*) or to stay open, just in the nick of time (*perceiving*).

Pairing the first two dimensions of personality with different dyads of perception-judgment facets yields 16 different personality types measured by the MBTI. Figure 7.3 presents a complete list of MBTI personality types.

Personality has been associated with job proficiency, career satisfaction, training proficiency, and even happiness (Lounsbury, Loveland, et al., 2003). For instance,

E/I	S/N	T/F	J/P
ISTJ	ISFJ	INFJ	INTJ
ISTP	ISFP	INFP	INTP
ESTP	ESFP	ENFP	ENTP
ESTJ	ESFJ	ENFJ	ENTJ

E = extraversion; I = introversion; S = sensing; N = intuition; T = thinking; F = feeling; J = judging; P = perceiving

Figure 7.3 MBTI personality types

Source: Myers-Briggs Type Indicator (MBTI) assessment.

results from a study of 500 ethnically diverse undergraduates revealed that Big-Five personality traits that were linked to happiness and happiness strategies (e.g., partying, religion, mental control, and goal pursuit) added significantly to the model's ability to explain differences in self-reported happiness (Tkach & Lyubomirsky, 2006). In other words, one's personality did not dictate or determine their level of happiness but rather personality influenced the frequency and nature of engagement in happiness strategies, which, in turn, was significantly linked to their self-reported happiness level.

Personality types, particularly the Big-Five personality traits, also have been linked to student performance in schools (Lounsbury, Gibson, Sundstrom, Wilburn, & Loveland, 2003), even among first-year college students (Lounsbury, Levy, Saudargas, & Gibson, 2006), and career decidedness (Lounsbury, Tatum, Chambers, Owens, & Gibson, 1999). For example, results from one study of 851 seventh, tenth, and twelfth graders demonstrated that Big-Five personality traits are related to career decidedness for middle and high school students too. Specifically, conscientiousness was positively and significantly associated with career decidedness in all three grades, while emotional stability was significant for 12th graders only (Lounsbury, Hutchens, & Loveland, 2005).

While useful, the literature discussed to this point has limits and elucidates only part of the underlying causal mechanism linking personality to college student success. There are other caveats that shape what we know about the influence of personality on student success generally and college students specifically. For instance, personality is fairly stable though it may vary from space to space. Just as definitions vary so too do lists of personality types from 16 types measured by the MBTI to over 4,000 identified by Allport (1985).

LITERATURE IN REVIEW

Now that we have reviewed the existing literature on personality, consider the following questions and answer them to the best of your ability.

1. How would you summarize what we know about personality?
2. Were you surprised by any major findings from research related to personality? If so, what were they and why were you surprised?
3. Describe how personality relates to academic success among college students in your own words.
4. Based on what you know about personality and its research base, is there theoretical support for the conclusions that the two professors made about "Geeta" in the opening story? YES or NO
5. What is your Myers-Briggs MBTI type? _____

A SHORT PERSONALITY TEST

Use the following scale to rate the extent to which you believe the following words or statements accurately reflect characteristics or aspects of your inner self:

	1 2 3 4 5 Disagree Agree Strongly Strongly
1. I am generally excited about things.	1 2 3 4 5
2. I experience anxiety frequently.	1 2 3 4 5
3. I prefer to go with my impulses often.	1 2 3 4 5

[1] **Extraversion**: scores below 3 may indicate "introversion," while scores of 3 and above may indicate "extraversion."
[2] **Neuroticism**: scores below 3 may indicate "emotional stability," while scores of 3 and above may indicate "emotional instability."
[3] **Conscientiousness**: scores below 3 may indicate "impulse control," while scores of 3 and above may indicate lack of such control.

Keep in mind that personality assessments are never based on single survey items so this short activity no doubt might suffer from measurement issues.

A Short Personality Test Activity

Consider the following questions using your scores from the activity as a guide:

1. Do you agree with your rating on extraversion? What evidence do you have that you're more or less extroverted?
2. Do you agree with your rating on neuroticism? How does your environment or situation influence your emotional stability level right now?
3. Do you agree with your rating on conscientiousness? How does the presence of others (e.g., friends, co-workers) influence your impulse control?

THEORY TO PRACTICE: A CASE STUDY

You've been hired by Mission University as an educational consultant who will work with the Vice President of Student Affairs to develop workgroups, each composed of three individuals, that will take steps over the next 18 months to implement the Division's strategic plan. The strategic plan has three major goals or objectives: (a) to use campus-based data in decisionmaking related to staffing, services, and resource allocation, (b) to enhance the "student experience" at Mission University by increasing student engagement in exciting, purposeful activities, and (c) to position the Division as a "national leader" among other institutions through creative, enterprising programs, especially new technological innovations.

To develop the three workgroups, you decide to use personality as a primary organizing unit. You convince the Vice President of the important role that personality plays in human behavior and gain approval to administer several personality assessments to student affairs staff at Mission. A private firm is responsible for scoring the instruments, but you are responsible for building a chart that outlines the personality types that likely flourish or perform optimally in work associated with each of the three strategic goals.

Case Study Activity

Using information from this chapter, complete the following matrix:

Workgroup	Goal	Personality Types	Related Facet
1	To use campus-based data in decisionmaking		
2	To enhance the "student experience" at Mission University		
3	To position the Division as a "national leader"		
EXAMPLE	*To maintain the status quo of Division*	*Agreeableness* *Conscientiousness*	*Trust* *Impulse control*

Feel free to list as many personality types as you'd like in the third column; list all that may apply. Use the fourth column to list facets, aspects, or specific examples of personality types. Figures 7.1, 7.2 and 7.3 may be helpful to you as you complete this exercise.

CONCLUSION

What's a textbook on social psychological theory without a chapter on personality? In my opinion, incomplete, which is why I devoted considerable space to this topic in the present volume. Personality is one term with many meanings. Some define it as the visible aspect of one's inner self, essence, or character, especially as perceived by others. Others refer to personality as a person's collection of qualities, the sum total of one's physical, mental, emotional, and social characteristics. Personality might also be thought of as the distinctive or essential character of a person (McCrae & Costa, 1997; Personality, 2003); and there are individual and common traits that comprise personality. Human behavior is a function of the interaction of the person and the environment (Lewin, 1951). Prior research supports a number of conclusions about personality: that it is generally stable, susceptible to social influence, and is associated with career decidedness, academic performance, and even happiness. There are multiple personality assessments such as the Myers-Briggs Type Indicator (MBTI) assessment and the Big-Five Personality Trait inventory. Personality is an important factor to consider when working in higher education contexts.

REFLECTIVE EXERCISES

1. Define positive psychology. (You should be a pro at this by now.)
2. Define personality.
3. What's the difference between personality and trait, if any?
4. List and briefly define one component of personality theory.
5. Place a mark closest to the word or phrase that most closely describes you:

	1	2	3	4	5	
a. Uses instinct						Uses logic
b. Bored by time alone						Need time alone
c. Chaotic						Organized

What do these scores or ratings say about your personality, in your opinion? Use language and terms from the chapter in your response.

CHAPTER SUMMARY

1. Personality is defined as the visible aspect of one's inner self, essence, or character, especially as perceived by others.
2. There are individual and common traits that comprise personality.
3. Human behavior is a function of the interaction of the person and the environment, according to Kurt Lewin, who advanced the equation:
   $B = f(P \times E)$.
4. Personality is generally stable, susceptible to social influence, and is associated with a number of important outcomes such as career decidedness, academic performance, and even happiness.
5. The Big-Five personality traits include: extraversion, agreeableness, openness, conscientiousness, and neuroticism.
6. The MBTI assessment yields 16 different combinations that represent distinct personality types.

DEFINITIONS

Use a dictionary to define the following terms or concepts that relate to personality:

agreeableness
character
conscientiousness
extraversion
introversion
neuroticism
personality

RESEARCH TIPS

1. Personality assessments are plentiful and in large supply. Some more valid than others. Nationally circulated instruments like the MBTI and Big-Five inventory can be used, for fee or with the author's permission, to assess the personality levels of higher education faculty, staff, and students.
2. Group differences in personality scores can be tested using a number of statistical techniques. For example, future researchers might determine if significant differences exist between two independent groups of college students (e.g., high-achievers and low-performers, athletes and non-athletes) using independent samples t-tests or analysis of variance when there are more than two groups.
3. Associations between personality scores and myriad measures of success can be tested using a number of statistical techniques. For example, future researchers might test the direction and magnitude of relations between students' personality scores and their grade point average (GPA) using bivariate correlations. One might even test the association between personality type (as defined by one's score on an assessment) and GPA, controlling for differences in time spent studying which is hypothesized to influence the GPA, using a hierarchical or sequential linear regression approach.

FURTHER READING

Ackerman, P.L., & Heggestad, E.D. (1997). Intelligence, personality, and interests: Evidence for overlapping traits. *Psychological Bulletin, 121*, 219–245.

Antony, J.S. (1998). Personality-career fit and freshman medical career aspirations: A test of Holland's theory. *Research in Higher Education, 39*, 679–698.

Baldwin, J.A. (1987). African psychology and Black personality testing. *Negro Educational Review, 38*(2–3), 56–66.

De Raad, B. (2000). *The Big Five personality factors: The psychological approach to personality*. Seattle, WA: Hogrefe & Huber.

Gosling, S.D., Rentfrow, P.J., & Swann, W.B. (2003). A very brief measure of the Big-Five personality domains. *Journal of Research in Personality, 37*(6), 504–528.

Niebuhr, R. (1996). *The nature and destiny of man*. Westminster: John Knox Press.

Srivastava, S., John, O.P., Gosling, S.D., & Potter, J. (2003). Development of personality in early and middle adulthood: Set like plaster or persistent change? *Journal of Personality and Social Psychology, 84*, 1041–1053.

REFERENCES

Allport, G.W. (1954). *The nature of prejudice*. Cambridge, MA: Addison-Wesley.

Allport, G.W. (1985). The historical background of social psychology. In G. Lindzey & E. Aronson (Eds.), *Handbook of Social Psychology* (Vol. 1, pp. 1–46). New York: Random House.

Barrick, M.R., & Mount, M.K. (1991). The Big Five personality dimensions and job performance: A meta-analysis. *Personnel Psychology, 44*, 1–26.

Cattell, R.B. (1950). *Personality: A systematic theoretical and factual study*. New York: McGraw-Hill.

John, O.P., & Srivastava, S. (1999). The Big-Five trait taxonomy: History, measurement, and theoretical perspectives. In L.A. Pervin & O.P. John (Eds.), *Handbook of personality: Theory and research* (Vol. 2, pp. 102–138). New York: Guilford Press.

Jung, C.G. (1971). *Psychological types*. Princeton, NJ: Princeton University Press.

Lewin, K. (1936). *Principles of topological psychology*. New York: McGraw-Hill.

Lewin, K. (1951). *Field theory in social science*. New York: Harper.

Lounsbury, J.W., Gibson, L.W., Sundstrom, E., Wilburn, D., & Loveland, J. (2003). An empirical investigation of the proposition that "School is Work": A comparison of personality-performance correlations in school and work settings. *Journal of Education and Work, 17*, 119–131.

Lounsbury, J.W., Hutchens, T., & Loveland, J.M. (2005). An investigation of Big Five personality trait and career decidedness among early and middle adolescents. *Journal of Career Assessment, 13*, 2–39.

Lounsbury, J.W., Levy, J.J., Saudargas, R.A., & Gibson, L.W. (2006). Big five personality traits and outcomes for first-year college students. *Journal of College Orientation and Transition, 14*, 62–68.

Lounsbury, J.W., Loveland, J.M., Sundstrom, E.D., Gibson, L.W., Drost, A.W., & Hamrick, F.L. (2003). An investigation of personality traits in relation to career satisfaction. *Journal of Career Assessment, 11*(3), 287–307.

Lounsbury, J.W., Tatum, H.E., Chambers, W., Owens, K., & Gibson, L.W. (1999). An investigation of career decidedness in relation to "Big Five" personality constructs and life satisfaction. *College Student Journal, 33*(4), 646–652.

McCrae, R.R., & Costa, P.T., Jr. (1997). Personality trait structure as a human universal. *American Psychologist, 52*, 509–516.

Personality. (2003). *Merriam-Webster's collegiate dictionary* (11th ed. Vol. 1). Springfield, MA: Encyclopedia Britannica.

Tkach, C., & Lyubomirsky, S. (2006). How do people pursue happiness? Relating personality, happiness-increasing strategies, and well-being. *Journal of Happiness Studies, 7*, 183–225.

8

MENTORING

Mutual Benefits, Separate Roles

Key Terms

antidote, common knowledge, dyad, mentoring, near-peer mentoring, peer mentoring, protégé, qualitative, quantitative

INTRODUCTION

Several years ago, I convened formal and informal focus groups of ethnically diverse college students at over 24 campuses across the country to talk about their academic and social experiences in college. I was particularly interested in identifying any barriers to their success, factors that seem to affect the likelihood of their retention in college, and ways in which they accessed resources to persist in college. There was great diversity among the group: some students were African American, others Latino; some were high achievers, sporting cumulative GPAs above 3.0; others were daily towing the line of academic dismissal. A few of the students in my group interview study were star athletes, others were gifted musicians, spoken word artists, gay student leaders, freelance tattoo artists, and even a "converted vegan . . . not vegetarian." Despite their differences in academic orientation, personal involvements, and, yes, dietary restrictions, one part of their response to my question about "resources they've accessed to succeed" converged on a single word: mentoring.

Although my graduate training focused almost exclusively on quantitative research methodologies by design, I have great respect for any perspective and most tools that enable us to see what was once concealed, understand that which continues to puzzle, or make the mundane marvelous, as I like to say. Qualitative methods, when executed appropriately, provide such deep insight. And as a hard-working student of qualitative methods—though clearly never a purist to the paradigm—I found the preponderance of comments about mentoring significant or should I say "thematic," saturating, and worthy of further investigation. So I asked my focus group participants to expound upon what they meant by mentoring, name to the extent possible what mentoring did for them, and offer illustrative examples of a "mentoring moment" they experienced.

Comments and experiences couldn't have been more different. Consider the following excerpts that provide fodder for the activities and exercises included in later sections of this chapter. Participants shared:

> A mentor is someone you can trust . . . at least mine is, but they're not like a friend. You've got to look up to them. (Student 1)
>
> My mentor is one of my academic advisors on campus. For some reason, she just took a noticeable interest in me my first year and she's been helping me out ever since. [Interviewer: Helping you as your academic advisor?] No, no . . . like doing other stuff and going beyond what she's paid for. She really reached out to me last year when I lost my grandmother and helped me work through personal stuff too. (Student 2)
>
> I guess it's hard for me to say because I have a lot of mentors . . . one for like every day of the week (laughing). I mean, it's not that bad, but I do have more than one mentor. One I go to talk about school stuff and they keep me on the straight and narrow. Another I stick with for church stuff and they also like help me think about my purpose. Then I got another one—it's like my only girl mentor—and we just met through my moms [sic] and she checks in more informally like. (Student 3)

Like any good research project, my work with these focus groups (and many others to come) left me with many more questions than answers. What's a mentor anyway? What makes mentoring work well? What do individuals derive from effective mentoring? And how might one explain this social phenomenon—that is, the process of mentoring? These questions are engaged in the present chapter, starting with a review of the existing literature, a discussion of core components related to mentoring, and a set of exercises to facilitate students' understanding of this information.

WHAT WE KNOW FROM MENTORING RESEARCH

The literature on mentoring is vast, spanning several decades, multiple disciplines, and various methodologies. A careful review of the extant literature reveals several major themes that relate to the focus of this chapter. First, much of what is written underscores the important role that mentoring plays in the academic and professional success of individuals, especially women and ethnic minorities who may face various forms of stress in majority settings. In fact, mentoring has been framed as an antidote to stress (Kram & Hall, 1989). Specifically, Kram and Hall analyzed data from 161 male managers and engineers within a large manufacturing company. They found that mentoring can be an important form of coping with stressful, unrewarding work conditions that characterize corporate downsizing and major organizational change. Additionally, early- and later-career professionals were as likely, or more likely than, midcareer colleagues to assume a mentoring role, contrary to popular belief or, shall I say, "common knowledge" (for more, see Chapter 1).

MENTORING AS AN ANTIDOTE FOR STRESS

Mentoring is a valuable resource for promoting learning and development, especially among college-age student populations. Mentoring has been framed as more than just a mechanism for stimulating personal and professional development of students, women, ethnic minorities, and professional staff; it holds promise as a powerful means of reducing stress arising from stressful and traumatic situations (Kram & Hall, 1989; Rodger & Tremblay, 2003). Evidence has shown that mentoring can provide those under stress with encouragement, guidance, coaching, advice, and meaningful support from experienced others.

Thinking about your own mentoring experiences, relationships, and what you know about the topic, respond to the following prompts with as much detail as possible.

1. Define mentoring in your own terms.
2. Name at least one individual who you consider to be your mentor and at least one way they've mentored you.
3. Name at least one individual for whom you've served as mentor and at least one way you've mentored them, if applicable.
4. Would you describe your mentoring relationship from #3 above as formal, informal, or a mix of both? Why? Explain citing a few examples.
5. Have you ever thought of mentoring as a remedy, or antidote, for stress? Can you recall a time when mentoring helped to reduce stress or trauma in your life?

Despite a long-standing belief in the importance of mentoring, there is considerable disagreement about its precise definition. Indeed a diversity of terms and definitions have been used to describe mentoring as a concept. For example, Healy (1997) posited that mentoring is "a dynamic, reciprocal relationship in a work environment between an advanced career incumbent (mentor) and a beginner (protégé) aimed at promoting the career development of both" (p. 10). On the other hand, Galbraith and Maslin-Ostrowski (2000) offered a different perspective that mentoring is "a process of intellectual, psychological, and affective development.... Mentors accept personal responsibility as competent and trustworthy non parental figures for the significant growth of other individuals" (pp. 136–137). Tallies can vary significantly; Jacobi (1991) cited over 15 definitions for mentoring, while Nora and Crisp (2007–2008) identified more than 30 definitions, each varying in scope and nature of one's roles. Much more information is needed to provide conceptual clarity in this area of our knowledge. (Free tip for interested students: This is a promising site for future thesis and dissertation research too, a real "gap" in the literature. Hint, hint.)

Different conceptualizations of mentoring have been proffered over time, implying different roles and responsibilities for mentors and protégés. For example, mentors often serve in multiple, at times conflicting, roles including role model, teacher (Galbraith & James, 2004), advisor, guide, resource, partner (Lee & Cramond, 1999), navigator (Biaggio, 2001), and even co-traveler (Hadjioannou, Shelton, Fu, & Dhanarattigannon,

2007), to name a few. And while most studies use these terms interchangeably, one study attempted to distinguish between them (Mertz, 2004). In her study, Mertz set forth a conceptual model of mentoring that differentiated between intent (e.g., role model, advisor, career advancement) and intensity of involvement (e.g., share dreams, trust, emotional investment). The intent and intensity of involvement determines the nature of the relationship and may distinguish job-related or contractual advising relations from close-knit role model arrangements that require personal investment. Taken together, the weight of evidence suggests that mentors and protégés assume different roles and expectations, engage one another in a number of ways, yet the roles and expectations shape what comes of one's mentoring experiences.

MY MENTORING CHECKLIST MANIFESTO

Mentoring has shown to be a valuable resource for individuals and an effective strategy for promoting learning, development, and success of both professional staff and college students. There's still some evidence, however, that some people struggle to identify appropriate mentors, engaged protégés, or ways to connect meaningfully with others in such arrangements.

PART A: Use the following scale to rate the extent to which you agree with each statement below. Then, in groups of at least two, share your results, compare answers, and discuss any differences and similarities among your responses.

1	2	3	4	5
NOT AT ALL		SOMETIMES		VERY MUCH

1. I would like to receive more mentoring from an experienced professional in my field.
2. The idea of being a mentor to others is appealing to me.
3. The quality of mentoring that I have received over the last year needs a good deal of improvement.
4. I firmly believe it is necessary to have a mentor in order to get ahead in this profession.
5. I prefer to be mentored by a peer or near-peer than to be mentored by an experienced, senior-level professional or colleague.
6. I have received mentoring from a faculty member or staff person on campus since enrolling in this program.
7. I feel like mentoring may be overrated.

PART B: Now, thinking back to your responses in Part A, respond to each of the following prompts as a way of developing your own mentoring checklist manifesto that offers some ideas about how you might take steps to develop new or enhance existing mentoring relations.

1. If you responded to the first statement above with a 2, 3, 4, or 5, what can you do, starting today, to access experienced professional mentors in your field or to signal your desire for such mentoring?
2. If you responded to the second statement above with a 2, 3, 4, or 5, what can you do, starting today, to make yourself available as a mentor to others or to signal your willingness to serve in that capacity?

3. If you responded to the third statement above with a 2, 3, 4, or 5, what can you do, starting today, to improve the quality of mentoring you receive?

   (a) With whom might you speak?
   (b) What needs to be shared?
   (c) What can you do to contribute to improving the quality?

4. If you responded to the fifth statement above with a 2, 3, 4, or 5, what can you do, starting today, to establish a mentoring relationship with a peer or near-peer?

   (a) Do you have someone particular in mind?
   (b) Have you reached out to them?
   (c) What are your goals and objectives for peer mentoring?

5. If you responded to the sixth statement above with a 1, what can you do, starting today, to connect with a faculty member or staff person on campus who might serve as a mentor for you?

   (a) Do you have someone in mind who you *know* has high expectations for you, believes in your abilities, and could impart knowledge and encouragement to you when needed?
   (b) What would be your role as protégé?

Mentors and protégés may engage one another both formally and informally (Welch, 1997). Formal mentoring refers to organized processes whereby knowledgeable and experienced persons directly engage in supportive ways with a less experienced person or protégé so as to facilitate his/her/hir development (Lee & Cramond, 1999). Formal mentoring often operates according to structured agreements, marked by intentional matching of mentoring dyads and guidelines specifying the frequency of meetings, accountability standards, and predetermined goals (Parise & Forret, 2008). Informal mentoring, on the other hand, refers to a more natural coming together of mentors and protégés—relationships that are far more organic, unstructured, casual, and spontaneous than formal relations. Informal mentoring typically requires no formal training, proceeds without defined duration, and can be marked by sporadic communication (Erickson, McDonald, & Elder, 2009).

Results are generally mixed about the impact of formal and informal mentoring on college students' development. For example, Strayhorn and Terrell (2007) analyzed College Student Experience Questionnaire (CSEQ) data from 554 Black collegians and found that meaningful, research-focused mentoring relationships with faculty positively influence Black students' satisfaction with college, whereas informal mentoring relations did not. We've also learned that some operational definitions of "formal" and "informal" mentoring vary from study to study, which confounds conclusions based on each type of arrangement.

Read the Strayhorn and Terrell (2007) study and then complete the following exercises:

1. Outline their argument for the study.
2. Take note of their sample and operational definition of mentoring.
3. Why do you think formal mentoring increased Black students' satisfaction with college?
4. Why not informal mentoring?
5. If you were directing a campus-based mentoring program, how might you use this information in your work with students?

PEER MENTORING QUIZ

1. What does peer mentoring mean to you?
2. What do you think are the most important elements of an effective peer mentoring program?
3. In terms of peer mentors, what knowledge, skills, or abilities do you think they should possess?

Peer mentoring also has shown effective for college students (Grant & Ensher, 2000) and business professionals (Allen, Russell, & Maetzke, 1997; Kram & Isabella, 1985), although much more information is needed about the profile of peer mentors, as well as the frequency and nature of peer mentoring relations that produce the outcomes we desire for students. For example, Rodger and Tremblay (2003) studied the effect of participation in a year-long peer mentoring program by analyzing data from 983 first-year university students who responded to the Academic Motivation Inventory. They found that peer-mentored students had significantly higher final grades than those who did not participate in the peer mentoring program. Similarly, mentoring seemed to mediate the influence of anxiety on academic performance, which generally reflects findings reported elsewhere (Kram & Hall, 1989).

Most mentoring programs operate under the assumption that those who participate in such programs are more likely than their peers who do not participate to succeed academically or professionally (Strayhorn & Saddler, 2009). For instance, Patitu and Terrell (1997) conducted a study to evaluate three components of the NASPA Minority Undergraduate Fellowship Program (MUFP) using data from 77 mentors and 76 protégés at 70 institutions. They found that MUFP was perceived to be effective for minority protégés, especially in terms of career exploration and skill development. As another example, Rose, Rukstalis, and Schuckit (2005) found that mentoring helped medical students excel, as mentors can be instrumental in conveying explicit academic knowledge required to master curriculum content.

Lastly, mentoring has been associated with positive outcomes for ethnic minorities in various fields and disciplines. For instance, mentoring has been shown to positively influence students' career decisions (Wanberg, Kammeyer-Mueller, & Marchese, 2006), socialization to professional roles, grades, retention during the first year of college, satisfaction with college, and even retention in science, technology, engineering, and math (STEM) fields (e.g., Cascio & Gasker, 2001; Kahveci, Southerland, & Gilmer, 2006; Strayhorn & Terrell, 2007). The weight of evidence suggests that "effective mentoring has assisted groups of people [especially African Americans] to advance socially, politically, and economically" (Redmond, 1990, p. 191). Multiple studies lend persuasive evidence to suggest that mentoring programs are an effective strategy for assisting students of color, such as African Americans, in higher education too (e.g., Patitu & Terrell, 1997; Strayhorn & Terrell, 2007).

Two final points deserve mention. First, contrary to popular beliefs or "common knowledge," mentoring does not always yield positive outcomes or go well for mentors or protégés; mentoring can have unhealthy aspects (Eby, McManus, Simon, & Russell, 2000). A small, but growing, line of inquiry in the corporate literature focuses on the nature and consequences of negative mentoring experiences (Eby, Durley, Evans, & Ragins, 2008; Simon & Eby, 2003), without much attention to the effect of imperfect matching or nonproductive interactions in higher education.

Second, prior research has shown, albeit inconsistently, that social identities can condition the formation and effectiveness of mentoring relations (Gaddis, 2012). It is clear that mentoring relationships that involve cross-racial or cross-gender pairings can be complex and difficult to initiate, maintain, and duplicate sometimes. That's not to say that all monoracial or same-sex mentoring pairs succeed either. Social identities can play a powerful role in mentoring and, for this reason, more postsecondary research is needed that explores the ways in which race, class, gender, and other personal characteristics shape what happens between mentors and protégés.

Taken together, the existing literature on mentoring serves as a useful conceptual framework for examining development of college students. Prior work suggests the importance of (a) type of mentoring (i.e., formal vs. informal), (b) frequency and mode of communication, (c) profile of mentor (e.g., faculty vs. peer), (d) impact of social identities on mentor–protégé dyads and (e) negative mentoring experiences. Figure 8.1 presents a graphical representation of this mentoring model that can be used in future higher education research and practice.

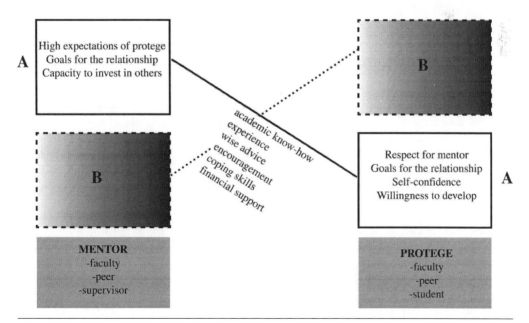

Figure 8.1

CONCLUSION

Indeed, mentoring is a valuable resource for promoting learning and development among college student populations. Research has shown that it has the *power* to offer encouragement to those in need, guidance to those in search of a path, and an antidote to those suffering under the weight of anxiety and stress. Mentoring has been associated with positive outcomes in college. Prior research and theory also has been useful for uncovering potential *problems* with mentoring as well. For instance, poor pairing can lead to unproductive or less effective mentoring. Cross-racial or cross-gender pairs may also present a number of challenges that shape the possibility of success. Information from this chapter can be used to understand mentoring as a concept, explain mentoring as social phenomenon, and assess its impact on students, as well as facilitate application of this information to practice in higher education and student affairs.

REFLECTIVE EXERCISES

Respond to the following questions to the best of your ability. Then, share your responses with others in groups of at least two (2) or in a large group/seminar setting.

1. What information from this chapter stood out for you?
2. What information from this chapter did you find most surprising?
3. What information from this chapter caught your attention and deserves further investigation? You might read the resources listed in "Further Reading" below.
4. What information from this chapter did you find "muddy" or deserving of additional clarification, explanation, illustration, or discussion?

CHAPTER SUMMARY

1. Mentoring is a valuable resource for promoting learning and development, especially among college-age student populations.
2. Mentoring has been framed as an antidote to stress.
3. Mentoring is "a dynamic, reciprocal relationship in a work environment between an advanced career incumbent (mentor) and a beginner (protégé) aimed at promoting the career development of both" (Healy, 1997, p. 10).
4. Most mentoring programs operate under the assumption that those who participate in such programs are more likely than their peers who do not participate to succeed academically or professionally.
5. Mentoring, when done well, provides mutual benefits to mentors and protégés. For more, see Figure 8.1.

DEFINITIONS

Working back through the chapter, develop a working definition of the following list of terms that relate to the study of social psychology, college student development theory, and mentoring.

antidote
common knowledge
dyad

mentoring
near-peer mentoring
peer mentoring
protégé
qualitative
quantitative

RESEARCH TIPS

1. Administer a survey to a group of students enrolled in Psychology 101 (or an equivalent undergraduate course that enrolls large numbers of students across academic majors) that includes items about the frequency (i.e., how often), nature (i.e., formal, informal, peer), and intent (e.g., career advancement) of their mentoring experiences. Pair this information with data about their academic performance: either self-reported grade point average (GPA) or grades from university transcripts. Conduct analyses to estimate the relationship between various aspects of mentoring (e.g., frequency) and college students' academic performance. Add rigor to your analysis by including statistical controls for factors that potentially confound this relationship such as age, sex, race/ethnicity, time spent studying, and academic major, to name a few.

2. Recruit students participating in a peer-mentoring program or informal peer-mentoring relations for one-on-one or group interviews. Develop an interview protocol that elicits information about their peer mentoring experiences, the profile and role of their peer mentor, how they understand their role as protégé, and what they perceive to gain from the peer-mentoring exchange. Figure 8.1 may serve as a useful heuristic or theoretical model for this proposed study.

FURTHER READING

Bernier, A., Larose, S., & Soucy, N. (2005). Academic mentoring in college: The interactive role of student's and mentor's interpersonal dispositions. *Research in Higher Education, 46*(1), 29–51.

Dawson, P. (2014). Beyond a definition: Toward a framework for designing and specifying mentoring models. *Educational Researcher, 43*(3), 137–145.

Gershenfeld, S. (2014). A review of undergraduate mentoring programs. *Review of Educational Research, 84*(3), 365–391.

Healy, C. C. (1997). An operational definition of mentoring. In H. T. Frierson, Jr. (Ed.), *Diversity in higher education* (pp. 9–22). Greenwich, CT: JAI Press.

Mertz, N. T. (2004). What's a mentor, anyway? *Educational Administration Quarterly, 40*(4), 541–560.

Strayhorn, T. L., & Terrell, M. C. (2007). Mentoring and satisfaction with college for Black students. *The Negro Educational Review, 58*(1–2), 69–83.

REFERENCES

Allen, T. D., Russell, J. E. A., & Maetzke, S. B. (1997). Formal peer mentoring: Factors related to protégés satisfaction and willingness to mentor others. *Group and Organizational Management, 22*(4), 488–507.

Biaggio, M. (2001). *Navigating roles in mentoring relationships with graduate students.* Paper presented at the annual conference of the American Psychological Association, San Francisco, CA.

Cascio, T., & Gasker, J. (2001). Everyone has a shining side: Computer-mediated mentoring in social work education. *Journal of Social Work Education, 37*(2), 283–293.

Eby, L. T., Durley, J. R., Evans, S. C., & Ragins, B. R. (2008). Mentors' perceptions of negative mentoring experiences: Scale development and nomological validation. *Journal of Applied Psychology, 93*(2), 358–373.

Eby, L. T., McManus, S. E., Simon, S. A., & Russell, J. E. A. (2000). The protégé's perspective regarding negative mentoring experiences: The developoment of a taxonomy. *Journal of Vocational Behavior, 57*, 1–21.

Erickson, L. D., McDonald, S., & Elder, G. H., Jr. (2009). Informal mentors and education: Complementary or compensatory resources? *Sociology of Education, 82*(4), 344–367.

Gaddis, S. M. (2012). What's in a relationship? An examination of social capital, race and class in mentoring relationships. *Social Forces, 90*(4), 1237–1269.

Galbraith, M. W., & James, W. B. (2004). Mentoring by the community college professor: One role among many. *Community College Journal of Research and Practice, 28*, 689–701.

Galbraith, M. W., & Maslin-Ostrowski, P. (2000). The mentor: Facilitating out-of-class cognitive and affective growth. In J. L. Bess & Associates (Eds.), *Teaching alone, teaching together* (pp. 133–150). San Francisco, CA: Jossey-Bass.

Grant, E. J., & Ensher, E. (2000). Effects of peer mentoring on types of mentor support, program satisfaction and graduate school success: A dyadic perspective. *Journal of College Student Development, 41*(6), 637–642.

Hadjioannou, X., Shelton, N. R., Fu, D., & Dhanarattigannon, J. (2007). The road to a doctoral degree: Co-travelers through a perilous passage. *College Student Journal, 41*(1), 160–177.

Healy, C. C. (1997). An operational definition of mentoring. In H. T. Frierson, Jr. (Ed.), *Diversity in higher education* (pp. 9–22). Greenwich, CT: JAI Press.

Jacobi, M. (1991). Mentoring and undergraduate student success: A literature review. *Review of Educational Research, 61*, 505–532.

Kahveci, A., Southerland, S. A., & Gilmer, P. J. (2006). Retraining undergraduate women in science, mathematics, and engineering. *Journal of College Science Teaching, 36*(3), 34–38.

Kram, K. E., & Hall, D. T. (1989). Mentoring as an antidote to stress during corporate trauma. *Human Resource Management, 28*(4), 493–510.

Kram, K. E., & Isabella, L. A. (1985). Mentoring alternatives: The role of peer relationships in career development. *Academy of Management Journal, 28*(1), 110–132.

Lee, J., & Cramond, B. (1999). The positive effects of mentoring economically disadvantaged students. *Professional School Counseling, 2*(3), 172–178.

Mertz, N. T. (2004). What's a mentor, anyway? *Educational Administration Quarterly, 40*(4), 541–560.

Nora, A., & Crisp, G. (2007–2008). Mentoring students: Conceptualizing and validating the multi-dimensions of a support system. *Journal of College Student Retention: Research, Theory & Practice, 9*(3), 337–356.

Parise, M. R., & Forret, M. L. (2008). Formal mentoring programs: The relationship of program design and support to mentors' perceptions of benefits and costs. *Journal of Vocational Behavior, 72*(2), 225–240.

Patitu, C. L., & Terrell, M. C. (1997). Participant perceptions of the NASPA Minority Undergraduate Fellows Program. *NASPA Journal, 17*(1), 69–80.

Redmond, S. (1990). Mentoring and cultural diversity in academic settings. *American Behavioral Scientist, 34*(2), 188–200.

Rodger, S., & Tremblay, P. F. (2003). The effects of a peer mentoring program on academic success among first year university students. *The Canadian Journal of Higher Education, 33*(3), 1–18.

Rose, G. L., Rukstalis, M. R., & Schuckit, M. A. (2005). Informal mentoring between faculty and medical students. *Academic Medicine, 80*(4), 344–348.

Simon, S. A., & Eby, L. T. (2003). A typology of negative mentoring experiences: A multidimensional scaling study. *Human Relations, 56*(9), 1083–1106.

Strayhorn, T. L., & Saddler, T. N. (2009). Gender differences in the influence of faculty-student mentoring relationships on satisfaction with college among African Americans. *Journal of African American Studies, 13*(4), 476–493.

Strayhorn, T. L., & Terrell, M. C. (2007). Mentoring and satisfaction with college for Black students. *The Negro Educational Review, 58*(1–2), 69–83.

Wanberg, C. R., Kammeyer-Mueller, J., & Marchese, M. (2006). Mentor and protégé predictors and outcomes of mentoring in a formal mentoring program. *Journal of Vocational Behavior, 69*(3), 410–423.

Welch, O. M. (1997). An examination of effective mentoring models in academe. In H. T. Frierson, Jr. (Ed.), *Diversity in higher education* (pp. 41–62). Greenwich, CT: JAI Press.

9

HOPE THEORY

Evidence of Things Not Seen . . .

Now faith is the substance of things hoped for and the evidence of things not seen.

—**Hebrews 11:1,** *King James Version*

We must accept finite disappointment but never lose infinite hope.

—**Dr. Martin Luther King, Jr.**

Key Terms

agency, aspirations, encouragement, faith, hope, negative psychology, pathways, positive psychology, optimism, trust

INTRODUCTION

Much of the positive psychology movement traces its origins to social psychology and social psychological theories (for more, see Chapter 1). As we've discussed, positive psychology is one branch of psychology that focuses on the scientific study of strengths and abilities that enable individuals and communities to excel, persist, thrive, or succeed. It's a counterpoint to more traditional psychology that has historically focused on studying determinants of pathology, psychosis, and suffering (Peterson, 2006; Seligman, 2004).

The difference between positive psychology and, might we say, "negative psychology" (i.e., traditional psychology) is more than semantics. Positive psychology has three targets: positive emotions, positive traits, and positive institutions. These are illustrated in Figure 9.1.

Let's consider a few examples. Positive emotions include confidence, trust, hope, and optimism; that is, feelings that sustain people in times of distress. Positive traits include strengths, virtues, and abilities such as intelligence, athleticism, and musical talents, to name a few. Democracy, family, church, and fraternity are examples of positive

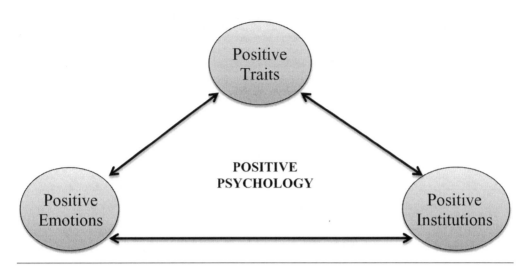

Figure 9.1 Targets of positive psychology

CORE TARGET	EXAMPLES
Positive emotions	confidence, courage, happiness, hope, optimism, trust, well-being
Positive institutions	church, community, democracy, family, fraternity
Positive traits	athleticism, charity, fairness, grit, intelligence, musicality, resilience, tenacity

Figure 9.2 Examples of positive psychology targets

institutions that provide support to individuals and communities in crisis or pain (Pajares, 2004; Seligman, 2012). Figure 9.2 presents a more complete summary.

A social psychological view of positive psychology concepts directs attention to the influence of the implied, imagined, or actual presence of others on one's level of hope, grit, tenacity, optimism, and so on. For instance, a social psychological approach to understanding hope moves from assessing just the degree to which individuals "feel like bad things will work out for them" to knowing how parents, peers, mentors, or spiritual figures influence one's hope for a better tomorrow.

In this chapter, we focus on hope theory as a social psychological theory and how it relates to our work in higher education. Before presenting core elements of hope theory, complete this short exercise and then let's reflect on one student's critical moment at a liberal arts college in Indiana.

A SHORT EXERCISE

Using this scale, respond to the following statements:	1 Not At All	2	3	4	5 Very Much
I meet goals that I set for myself.	1	2	3	4	5
I believe bad things will work out well.	1	2	3	4	5
I feel that I have a purpose in life.	1	2	3	4	5

Now, add up your ratings or scores on each of the three items above. Write your total score below and use the following guide to interpret your overall response.

Total Score:_____

[1] **Total scores ranging 3–7**: low hope; generally pessimistic, marked by feeling of hopelessness or out of one's control.

[2] **Total scores ranging 8–12**: medium hope; vacillates between periods of optimism and pessimism, glass may be half-full today and half-empty tomorrow, experiences lack of feelings of fulfillment about one's goals.

[3] **Total scores ranging 13–15**: high hope; generally optimistic, confident in one's future and an ability to control it.

A MOMENT TO REFLECT

On May 3, 2011, Tasha Jackson, an African American female, was ushered to the main stage at Earlham College's spring commencement by her best friend, Gavin Knox. Gavin, a graduating computer scientist, cherished many sweet memories of pushing Tasha in her *Norco* wheelchair during their years in college. During first-year orientation. At the junior college prom. But perhaps no memory as sweet as this. Tasha was about to speak at the university's commencement in front of thousands.

After four years of hard work, some sleepless nights of dizzying study, and over a dozen life-threatening surgeries to treat her debilitating illness, Tasha had reached the finish line of her college goal: she was about to graduate summa cum laude in the top 1% of her class. After the university's ensemble led the unrehearsed group through the most elegant version of the school's alma mater that was possible without screening out "bad singers" at the door, the Provost introduced Tasha and invited her to the podium. Nervous but convinced that her speech would turn out well if she could just fight back the tears, Tasha began:

> Today marks the end of a remarkable past and the beginning of an even brighter future. The past was remarkable because we shared it together. There were losses. But many more victories. We faced challenges. But we overcame great challenges with impressive courage and unwavering strength. Our individual wins are worthy but it's our collective achievements that tie us. Indeed, the past four years were remarkable because we shared them together.
>
> Today also marks the beginning of an even brighter future. Many have asked me questions about my physical condition. Does it hurt? Are you in pain? Will the pain ever go away? Initially I found these probes difficult because there has surely been hurt and pain. But over time, I found refuge and relief in good things: good times with friends like Gavin, holidays well spent with family, and the welcoming campus community that we call "The Earlham Family."
>
> Still true relief from my suffering didn't come until I found my purpose, my passion, and meaning in my experiences at Earlham. I imagine a world where one's acceptance does not depend on his or her ability status. That world does not yet exist, but I've seen hints of it in my time here at Earlham. I envision schools where teachers pay attention to students' learning needs and happily accommodate those of us living with disabilities. That wasn't my experience in high school, but I've felt supported and like I belong here at Earlham. Our time together at Earlham has given me hope for a brighter tomorrow. Today is the beginning of that brighter future for me, for you, for us all. Congratulations fellow graduates and thank you for being *the evidence of things I've not yet seen. . . .*

As Tasha wheeled off stage left, the entire auditorium erupted in thunderous applause with unanimous ovation. She was correct: her speech turned out well. And many in the audience were inspired by her words.

A REFLECTIVE EXERCISE

Respond to the following questions to the best of your ability.

1. How do you feel *about* the content of Tasha's commencement address?
2. How do you feel *after reading* Tasha's commencement address?
3. Now complete the following exercise:

Using this scale, respond to the following statements:	1 Not At All	2	3	4	5 Very Much
There are many ways around problems.	1	2	3	4	5
I believe bad things can work out well.	1	2	3	4	5
Purpose in life can relieve suffering.	1	2	3	4	5

4. Compute your total score by adding up your rating on each item. Was your total score on this exercise *greater than* your score from "A Short Exercise"? YES or NO
5. What role, if any, do you think Tasha's commencement speech played in changing your score?

CORE ELEMENTS OF THE THEORY

Recall that Tasha ended her commencement address by invoking an excerpt from Christian scriptures: "the evidence of things hoped for . . ." (Hebrews 11:1). What is hope after all? Hope is generally defined as the perceived ability to clearly conceptualize one's goals and derive paths to achieve them. Hope is a feeling of anticipation, that some desire will be satisfied, or a promise will be fulfilled despite delay, setbacks, or trouble (Snyder, 2000).

Hope has three primary components according to theory: goals, pathways, and agency (Snyder, 2000). *Goals* refers to setting objectives or aims for one's life. *Pathways* refers to finding various ways to achieve goals and objectives. *Agency* is the belief that one can act or do something to achieve desired goals. These components are additive, dynamic, and reciprocal but not synonymous (Snyder, 1994, 1995).

Beyond this, hope is believed to have four constitutive elements: mastery, attachment, survival, and spiritual. Mastery, for example, refers to priorities and feelings of control. Attachment, on the other hand, includes feelings of trust and openness. Spirituality, though often confused with religion, is a broader concept that relates to meaning and purpose in life (Scioli & Biller, 2009). Figure 9.3 presents a summary of these elements.

QUOTABLE MOMENT

The capacity for hope is the most significant fact of life. It provides human beings with a sense of destination, and the energy to get started.
—Norma Cousins, American journalist

CORE ELEMENT	EXAMPLES
Mastery	control, priorities
Attachment	support, disclosure
Survival	trust, calm
Spirituality	meaning, purpose

Figure 9.3 Four core elements of hope

Source: Information supported by research from Synder (2000).

A POP QUIZ

Our discussion of positive psychology and hope is moving rapidly. Already we've covered the connection between positive psychology and hope, a few exercises and scales, and the core elements of the model. Before proceeding to a review of existing literature and application to higher education practice, here's a pop quiz (you'll thank me later):

1. What's positive psychology in your own words?
2. What's the goal of traditional or "negative" psychology in your own words?
3. Name at least three constructs from positive psychology.
4. Complete the following: "Now faith is the substance of _____."
5. What's your own personal interpretation of the quote in #4 above that also opened this chapter?
6. And how does it relate to your work in higher education?
7. Define hope according to Charles Richard Snyder.
8. Now define hope in your own words.

WHAT WE KNOW FROM RESEARCH

Contrary to popular belief, intelligence or "IQ" (intelligence quotient) is not the only or primary determinant of student success in educational settings. Even gifted and talented people fail to achieve academically and we all know "that student" who is brighter than the sun but performs poorly on tests, gets low grades, and may have dropped out of school altogether. It is clear that more than intelligence matters and the weight of empirical evidence suggests that we want to know more.

Extensive research has been directed at identifying factors that promote or inhibit academic achievement among students. A long line of studies has shown the importance of academic skills, readiness, or performance. Yet, academic factors account for only about 25% of the variance in most postsecondary academic outcomes (Strayhorn, 2013).

A separate line of inquiry demonstrates the importance of motivational factors such as self-efficacy and optimism. For instance, we've learned that self-efficacy is domain-specific (Bandura, 1997; Lent, Brown, & Larkin, 1986). So students' confidence in their academic skills (e.g., their ability to write class essays) predicts success in completion of academic tasks such as earning good grades, completing assignments, or graduating to higher levels of education such as graduate study (Chemers, Hu, & Garcia, 2001; Poyrazli, Arbona, Nora, McPherson, & Pisecco, 2002; Strayhorn, 2010). And academic confidence does not necessarily provide the confidence needed to drive well.

While useful, the literature discussed to this point has limits and elucidates only part of the underlying causal mechanism in student success. Other social psychological factors like hope matter. Hope is defined as "the process of thinking about one's goals, along with the motivation to move toward these goals (agency) and the ways to achieve those goals (pathways)" (Snyder, 1995, p. 355). And it's the ability to conceive or generate multiple pathways to achieve desired goals that may give students a sense of hope or control over their academic destinations and educational outcomes. A good deal of attention has been devoted to discerning differences between hope, its constitutive elements and other factors like resilience. See Figure 9.4 for a summary.

STRENGTHS +	VIRTUES =	RESILIENCE
Grit	Fairness	Buoyancy
Tenacity	Charity	"Bounce back"
Intelligence	Justice	Success
Athleticism	Duty	
Musicality	Optimism	

Figure 9.4 Formula for hope

Hope has predicted final grades in a college psychology course (Snyder, 1994; Snyder et al., 1991), even after controlling for scores on initial quizzes and exams. Hope has also been compared to optimism in predicting life satisfaction; results indicate that hope (agency) is a stronger predictor of "the good life" than optimism (Bailey, Eng, Frisch, & Snyder, 2007). The positive relationship between hope and academic success in college is another major finding from previous research. For example, Snyder and colleagues (2002) analyzed survey data from 213 freshman students at a Midwestern university and found that hope predicted GPA, course grades, and academic dismissal over a six-year period. Positive associations between hope and success in college persisted even after controlling for college entrance exam scores.

A final category of "hope research" is composed of studies that test the development and validation of surveys or scales to assess individuals' level of hope. For instance, *The Hope Scale* has been tested and validated on adult samples (Snyder et al., 1991). The Hope Scale consists of four agency items, four pathways items, and four filler or placebo-like items that measure neither construct. Modifications of this scale have been developed for kids by Snyder et al. (1997) and other groups by others (Scioli & Biller, 2009). Generally, scales demonstrate adequate alpha reliability (alphas averaging 0.92) and all subscales have reliabilities that exceed 0.70. Here are a few sample items drawn from hope scales available in the public domain (Scioli & Biller, 2009; Snyder, 2000):

1. Every day I feel closer to my goals.
2. I am able to rely on others to achieve my goals.
3. I have used prayer to accomplish a goal.
4. I can find lots of ways around any problem.
5. I achieve the goals that I set for myself.

LITERATURE IN REVIEW

Now that we have reviewed the existing literature on hope, consider the following questions and answer them to the best of your ability.

1. How would you summarize what we know about hope?
2. Were you surprised by any major findings from research related to hope? If so, what were they and why were you surprised?
3. Describe how hope promotes academic success among college students in your own words. (Hint: Use "agency" and "pathways" in your response.)

RESEARCH NOTE: NARRATIVE ANALYSIS

Extending Clandinin and Connelly's (2000) comments about the purpose and nature of narrative research, Creswell (2003) described narrative inquiry as "a form of inquiry in which the researcher studies the lives of individuals and asks one or more individuals to provide stories about their lives. This information is then told and retold or restoried by the researcher into a narrative chronology. In the end, the narrative combines views from the participant's life with those of the researcher's life in a collaborative narrative" (p. 15).

Generally speaking, there are at least five forms of narrative inquiry. They include (Marshall & Rossman, 2006):

1. life histories
2. biographies
3. autobiographies
4. oral histories
5. personal narratives

Narrative inquiry makes a number of assumptions that inform the tradition. For example, narrative inquiry is all about stories—"storytelling is integral to understanding lives" (Marshall & Rossman, 2006, p. 6). It's also assumed that people construct stories as a way of creating and re-creating identity. Lastly, narrative analysis focuses on sociolinguistic techniques (i.e., *how* the story is told), life events that affect the storyteller, and the meaning they make of such experiences.

All this is not to equate the rigors of narrative inquiry with the ease of gossip, fables, or good ole [fictitious] storytelling. Narrative inquiry is method. It begins with eliciting the story in the words, time, and space of the teller's voice. This method also elicits vivid description of time, place, plot, and scene, including depictions of characters and physical environments. While this information may be difficult to draw out and even more difficult to produce (on the part of the teller), it is essential to narrative inquiry and may be as "informing as an old gossip" (Welty, 1979, p. 163).

ANALYZING TASHA'S HOPE NARRATIVE

Before we continue to other activities that allow us to use what we've learned about hope, let's turn back to Tasha's commencement speech that appeared earlier in the chapter under "A Moment to Reflect." Respond to the following meaningfully:

1. Reread the 1st paragraph *only* under "A Moment to Reflect." Do not go on to #2 below until you've reread the entire first paragraph under that section.
2. With just the 1st paragraph in mind, what are your thoughts about Tasha? And your thoughts or prior knowledge about Earlham College?
3. Now, reread the 2nd paragraph under "A Moment to Reflect."
4. How have your thoughts about Tasha changed as a result of what you read in the 2nd paragraph? And to what do you attribute the change?
5. Now reread the 3rd paragraph under "A Moment to Reflect," which is the 1st paragraph of Tasha's speech. What words or phrases signal "hope" in your opinion?
6. Is Tasha's perspective of the past generally positive or generally negative? And how does that compare to most college students you know or with whom you work?
7. Now reread the 4th paragraph under "A Moment to Reflect," which is the 2nd paragraph of Tasha's speech. How does Tasha make meaning of her experiences? How does she relate "relief" from pain to good times?
8. Given your response in #7 above, how might you use this information when working with a hurting or suffering student?

FEAR OF PUBLIC SPEAKING

It is estimated that 5.3 million Americans have a social phobia or fear. Social phobias vary in type. Here are three common types:

1. Acrophobia: fear of heights.
2. Arachnophobia: fear of spiders.
3. Claustrophobia: fear of enclosed spaces.

Another type of phobia that is less well known by its actual name is glossophobia, or fear of public speaking. Estimates vary but some have argued that anywhere from 19 to 60% of people suffer from speech anxiety. Glossophobia is known by other names too: stage fright, performance anxiety, and social anxiety disorder.

There are several causes of glossophobia. One primary cause is lack of preparation. Others include:

1. Overthinking the moment.
2. Being or feeling underprepared.
3. Worrying about the inevitable or uncontrollable.
4. Fretting that things will fail or go badly.

Just as there are multiple factors or experiences that may lead to glossophobia, there are several proven ways to reduce, if not eliminate, speech anxiety. Next time you feel your mouth getting excessively dry, you're overwhelmed with worry about your talk, or your mind starts racing before a speech, try the following strategies:

1. Think beyond the present moment.
2. Think positively and stay focused on your goal to do well.
3. Contemplate pathways to achieving your goal of a successful speech (e.g., how will you begin/opening line? How will you end? What's the punch line?)
4. Anticipate problems that might arise with timing, technology, and setting.
5. Most of all, prepare.
6. And, if needed, rub the inside of your palm with the opposite thumb; this is known to calm nerves and senses when anxiety levels are high.

THEORY TO PRACTICE: A CASE STUDY

A Hope in the Unseen

Pulitzer prize-winning author, Ron Suskind (1999), wrote this novel as a narrative or story about Cedric Jennings, a gifted young Black male who grew up in the urban, inner-city of Washington, DC. Cedric attended Ballou High School, a failing school located in the southeast corridor of the district. Suskind, a *Wall Street Journal* reporter, follows Cedric through his last two years of high school and his freshman year at an Ivy League institution, Brown University.

It's clear from the very first page that Cedric faces seemingly insurmountable odds stacked against him. A tenuous relationship with his ex-con, drug-dealing dad. A hard-working but poorly paid mom, Barbara, who insists on Cedric "keeping his nose clean" by staying out of trouble. And unrelenting harassment and dehumanizing teasing by peers at school for his boundless optimism and determined academic focus. Despite setbacks, Cedric maintains hope in the unseen—what he's never seen and few think even possible—high performance amidst complacency, success borne from failure, and a path out of the inner city to the Ivy League. It's a blend of his mother's courage, a passion for math, fiery Pentecostal sermons, and inspirational Black music with his unwavering faith in the future that empowers him at low moments, comforts him in trouble, and inspires him to believe that, despite all evidence to the contrary, something better awaits him if he keeps the courage to fight for it. This story of triumph and perseverance is a must read for anyone interested in the concept of hope.

Case Study Activity

1. Locate a copy of Suskind's *A Hope in the Unseen* and read it.
2. Create reading groups (i.e., 2–3 people) or communities of practice to discuss the book, Suskind's underlying thesis, and Cedric's amazing capacity to hold on in the face of unexpected setbacks and obstacles.

3. Use some of the information presented in "Research Note: Narrative Analysis" to analyze Cedric's story, how it relates to hope, and your work with college students.
4. If it's the ability or capacity to conceive pathways to a desired end that gives one hope, then what do you think enabled Cedric's capacity to do so?
5. Think about how sharing a copy of the book with one of your students might positively influence their own courage to hope in things unseen.

CONCLUSION

By now, we've spent a good deal of time thinking about hope and hope theory as they relate to college students, their success, and our work with them as educators. Hope is generally defined as the perceived ability to clearly conceptualize one's goals and derive paths to achieve them. Hope is a feeling of anticipation, that some desire will be satisfied, or a promise will be fulfilled despite delay, setbacks, or trouble (Snyder, 2000). Information contained in this chapter serves as a primer, of sorts, for those interested in positive psychology, social psychological derivatives of that movement, and how students build and use hopeful optimism as a bridge to their desired end.

REFLECTIVE EXERCISES

1. Define positive psychology.
2. Define hope.
3. What's the difference between hope and optimism?
4. What proportion of variance in postsecondary academic outcomes is explained by academic variables like grades, test scores, and GPA?
5. List and briefly define the three primary components of hope theory.
6. What commonalities do you see between the narratives of Tasha Jackson and Cedric Jennings?

CHAPTER SUMMARY

1. Positive psychology is one branch of psychology that focuses on the scientific study of strengths and abilities that enable individuals and communities to excel, persist, thrive, or succeed.
2. Positive psychology has three targets: positive emotions, positive traits, and positive institutions.
3. Hope is generally defined as the perceived ability to clearly conceptualize one's goals and derive paths to achieve them.
4. Hope has three primary components according to theory: goals, pathways, and agency.
5. Hope has four constitutive elements: mastery, attachment, survival, and spiritual.
6. Academic factors or variables account for only about 25% of the variance in most postsecondary achievement outcomes.

7. It's the ability to conceive or generate multiple pathways to achieve desired goals that may give students a sense of hope or control over their academic destinations and educational outcomes.

8. The Hope Scale consists of four agency items, four pathways items, and four filler items that measure neither agency nor pathways.

DEFINITIONS

Use a dictionary to define the following terms or concepts that relate to hope:

agency
aspirations
encouragement
faith
hope
negative psychology
pathways
positive psychology
optimism
trust

RESEARCH TIPS

1. Hope is a relatively new area of research in higher education.

2. Survey data can be analyzed with path analysis or structural equation modeling to test the hypothesized structure of hope. For instance, survey items can be developed to assess hope components such as goals or pathways. Appropriate analytic methods can then be used to determine whether items represent separate factors and the interrelationships between hope factors.

3. Narrative inquiry is a well-respected approach to qualitative research. As this chapter demonstrates, it has enormous potential for studying hope, its drivers, and hope as it is deployed to overcome obstacles. Future researchers are encouraged to build upon information from this chapter to conduct narrative studies with college students in the future.

FURTHER READING

Bailey, T.C., Eng, W., Frisch, M.B., & Snyder, C.R. (2007). Hope and optimism as related to life satisfaction. *The Journal of Positive Psychology, 2*(3), 168–175.

Scioli, A., & Biller, H.B. (2009). *Hope in the age of anxiety: A guide to understanding and strengthening our most important virtue.* Oxford: Oxford University Press.

Seligman, M.E.P. (2012). *Flourish: A visionary new understanding of happiness and well-being.* New York: Atria Books.

Snyder, C.R. (1994). *The psychology of hope: You can get here from there.* New York: Free Press.

Snyder, C.R. (Ed.). (2000). *Handbook of hope: Theory, measures, and applications.* New York: Academic Press.

Strayhorn, T.L. (2009). Different folks, different hopes: The educational aspirations of Black males in urban, suburban, and rural high schools. *Urban Education, 44*(6), 710–731.

REFERENCES

Bailey, T.C., Eng, W., Frisch, M.B., & Snyder, C.R. (2007). Hope and optimism as related to life satisfaction. *The Journal of Positive Psychology, 2*(3), 168–175.

Bandura, A. (1997). *Self-efficacy: The exercise of control.* New York: Freeman.

Chemers, M.M., Hu, L., & Garcia, B.F. (2001). Academic self-efficacy and first year college student performance and adjustment. *Journal of Educational Psychology, 93*(1), 55–64.

Clandinin, D.J., & Connelly, F.M. (2000). *Narrative inquiry: Experience and story in qualitative research.* San Francisco: Jossey-Bass.

Creswell, J.W. (2003). *Research design: Qualitative, quantitative, and mixed methods approaches* (2nd ed.). Thousand Oaks, CA: Sage.

Lent, R.W., Brown, S.D., & Larkin, K.C. (1986). Self-efficacy in the prediction of academic performance and perceived career options. *Journal of Counseling Psychology, 33*(3), 265–269.

Marshall, C., & Rossman, G.B. (2006). *Designing qualitative research.* Thousand Oaks, CA: Sage Publications.

Pajares, F. (2004). Toward a positive psychology of academic motivation. *The Journal of Educational Research, 90,* 27–35.

Peterson, C. (2006). *A primer in positive psychology.* Oxford: Oxford University Press.

Poyrazli, S., Arbona, C., Nora, A., McPherson, R., & Pisecco, S. (2002). Relation between assertiveness, academic self-efficacy, and psychosocial adjustment among international graduate students. *Journal of College Student Development, 43*(5), 632–642.

Scioli, A., & Biller, H.B. (2009). *Hope in the age of anxiety: A guide to understanding and strengthening our most important virtue.* Oxford: Oxford University Press.

Seligman, M.E.P. (2004). *Authentic happiness: Using the new positive psychology to realize your potential for lasting fulfillment.* New York: Atria Books.

Seligman, M.E.P. (2012). *Flourish: A visionary new understanding of happiness and well-being.* New York: Atria Books.

Snyder, C.R. (1994). *The psychology of hope: You can get here from there.* New York: Free Press.

Snyder, C.R. (1995). Conceptualizing, measuring, and nurturing hope. *Journal of Counseling & Development, 73,* 355–360.

Snyder, C.R. (Ed.). (2000). *Handbook of hope: Theory, measures, and applications.* New York: Academic Press.

Snyder, C.R., Harris, C., Anderson, J.R., Holleran, S.A., Irving, L.M., Sigmon, S.T., & et al. (1991). The will and the ways: Development and validation of an individual-differences measure of hope. *Journal of Personality and Social Psychology, 60,* 570–585.

Snyder, C.R., Hoza, B., Pelham, W.E., Rapoff, M., Ware, L., Danovsky, M., & et al. (1997). The development and validation of the Children's Hope Scale. *Journal of Pediatric Psychology, 22,* 399–421.

Snyder, C.R., Shorey, H.S., Cheavens, J., Pulvers, K.M., Adams, V.H., III, & Wiklund, C. (2002). Hope and academic success in college. *Journal of Educational Psychology, 94*(4), 820–826.

Strayhorn, T.L. (2010). Buoyant believers: Resilience, self-efficacy, and academic success of low-income African American collegians. In T.L. Strayhorn & M.C. Terrell (Eds.), *The evolving challenges of black college students: New insights for policy, practice, and research* (pp. 49–65). Sterling: Stylus Publishing.

Strayhorn, T.L. (2013). Academic achievement: A higher education perspective. In J. Hattie & E. Anderman (Eds.), *International guide to student achievement* (pp. 16–18). New York: Routledge.

Suskind, R. (1999). *A hope in the unseen: An American odyssey from the inner city to the ivy league.* New York: Broadway Books.

Welty, E. (1979). *The eye of the story: Selected essays and reviews.* New York: Vintage Books.

10

SOCIAL INFLUENCE

How Others Shape Us and Our Aspirations

People cannot attain what they do not dream (or think possible).

—**Deborah Faye Carter (2001, p. 6)**

It's impossible to achieve that which you cannot see or ever hope to become that which you've never seen. You're responsible for what you see.

—**Terrell Lamont Strayhorn**

Key Terms

aspirations, expectations, goals, identity development motivation, self-authorship, social capital, social influence, social psychology

INTRODUCTION

Long after I thought this book was finished, I realized the need for this additional chapter that focuses on social influence and the power that the implied, imagined, or actual presence of others plays on one's aspirations, hopes, and dreams for the future. As you might imagine, there were many signals that the manuscript deck, so to speak, was one card away from full. For instance, students would share in my interview studies that they were inspired to attend college by meeting someone who had gone to college and their personal testimony alone compelled some youth to believe they could do the same.

Other students talked about the influence of fictitious characters, like actors from *A Different World* or *School Daze* (a TV sitcom and movie, respectively), whose mere presence on an imagined campus provoked new interest in attending college or sustained their existing interest in doing so. Still others would share how they were socialized or raised by parents or guardians who had every expectation that the student would attend college and ultimately graduate; for them, college attendance was both satisfying parental expectations and obeying their parents' wishes. Indeed, individuals are power-fully influenced by others and the magnitude of that influence is determined, at least in part, by a host of social factors (e.g., proximity) and the nature of their social connection to one another.

Give it a try. Look at someone and yawn. What do they do in return? Yawn. If you're reading this chapter in the presence of others, catch someone's attention nearby and start rubbing your nose incessantly. What do they do in return? Presto, they start rubbing their nose even if it's not itching. Go to a crowded coffee shop, sit down, and stare at someone across the room. Once you have their attention (usually accompanied by eye-rolling or furtive glances left-and-right while they determine if you're *actually* staring at them), start wiggling your foot. What do they do in return? You guessed it; they wiggle their foot back at you. Why does all of this occur so *naturally*? Because social influence is part of human behavior and individuals are powerfully influenced by others.

With every new revelation affirming the importance of this topic, I would find myself deeply involved in a conversation with a student, colleague, or friend about the enormity of my discovery—that any treatment of social psychological theory in higher education must address the role of social influence and any discussion of educational aspirations that fails to mention the social influence factor is incomplete. Usually in full agreement, my friends and listeners would chime in saying: "Yes, that's true . . . but that's kind of common sense, right? That we all influence each other." This refrain underscored that this topic deserved its own place in the book since, by now I hope you realize, that common sense is anything *but common* (knowledge to all). In fact, many "common sense" claims are nonsense, non-scientific, and oftentimes just plain false-dot-com, as I like to say.

Let me restate a previous example that challenges the "commonsense" assumption that one must be present to influence another. Remember from Chapter 1 that I intro-duced my study of Black students in campus gospel choirs (Strayhorn, 2011). Through that project, I met a young man whose mother passed away while he was a freshman in college. Though deceased and, thus, *physically not present*, her imagined presence powerfully influenced the young man and motivated him to persist in college despite academic setbacks, emotional stresses, and his own willingness to quit. He would say things like: "I just believe she's watching me and telling me to hang in there, so I can't give up . . . I gotta [sic] finish school." In short, imaginal or absent (but known) figures can powerfully influence our actions by shaping how we experience events, our inter-pretation of those events, and the meaning we attach to them. And though imagined or physically *not present*, their influence on our behaviors can be just as real as the touch of one who is standing in front of us. Remember, commonsense might be reduced to *non-sense* when you evaluate the validity of such claims using extant research and theory.

And over the course of this volume, I have outlined several beliefs or assumptions that masquerade as facts or commonsense when they are actually false, nonsense, and consistently unconfirmed by research. Consider the following as examples:

1. Men exhibit more hostility toward women than women do toward men.
2. People who are paid a lot of money and work-related benefits to perform a bor-ing task enjoy it much more than those who are paid little to no money.

3. To detect people's lies, you should pay close attention to their faces.
4. Physically attractive people are presumed more intelligent than those deemed physically unattractive.
5. The more bystanders there are to a crime or accident, the more likely a victim is to be helped or aided.
6. Students whose self-esteem is contingent upon their performance in academic tasks tend to feel "at home" and less anxious in challenging learning environments.
7. College students who feel as if they belong in college always perform better than those who "stick out" and do *not* feel as if they belong.

While interesting and perhaps *plausibly* or *reasonably* true, each of these statements is false and unsupported by research findings. There is no correlation between the number of bystanders to a crime or accident and the probability of a victim being helped or aided, just as there is no correlation between attractiveness and intelligence or IQ. In fact, most research suggests that a victim is less likely to be helped or aided when there are more bystanders or witnesses to a crime—everyone assumes someone else will do it. You see even in our propensity to help others we are influenced by the imagined, actual, or implied presence of others. Nevertheless, social influence is important and we are remarkably influenced by those around us and those to whom we are socially related.

WHAT'S COMMON KNOWLEDGE, AGAIN?

Have you ever used the phrase "common knowledge" to refer to some taken-for-granted truth or fact that's alleged to be so obvious that it needs no explanation or support? For instance, rich people have more money. Is this a valid and true statement? Any invitation for explanation is likely to seem fruitless or circular in thinking as most would just say, "Sure, that's common knowledge." A dog is a man's best friend. But why and on what basis? Here again individuals are rarely compelled to produce generalizable evidence to support such claims. In fact, they are so pervasive that many of them show up in media, social media, and casual conversations without introduction or defense. It's just "common knowledge," as we like to say.

The term common knowledge was derived from David Hume's (1740) thoughts about the social nature of knowledge. Hume was perhaps the first to make reference to explicit knowledge and the importance of mutual knowledge, or knowledge that's shared by many if not all. Yet, it was likely David Lewis (1969) who was first to offer an explicit analysis of "common knowledge," per se. And what we've learned from earlier works in sociology, psychology, and literary studies is that common knowledge is important in social interactions, often assumed without critical analysis, and what's common knowledge for some may be not-so-common for all. Interrogating common knowledge about social interactions, social behaviors, and beliefs is one of the primary goals of social psychology.

Consider the classic example of the clumsy waiter. It's a busy weekend night at a popular and buzzing new restaurant in town. A male waiter, pressed to keep pace with the flow of customers, moves briskly by several tables, slips, and spills dark gravy on a dining guest's white evening gown. Stunned and embarrassed, the guest looks at her new dress in complete disbelief, opens her eyes wider than ever to take in the full effect of this *accident* (or, for our purposes, social interaction), and then glares at the waiter through heated, squinted eyes. Immediately, the waiter says: "I'm so sorry . . . it's all my fault."

Why did the waiter announce that it was his fault? Isn't this obvious or *common knowledge*? If one is dining in a restaurant and a hurried waiter spills gravy on a guest, then is there ever a time when it wouldn't be the waiter's fault? Some would say no—customers are always right. But the waiter's announcement of the so-called obvious implies that there *must be* conditions (no matter how unobvious to others) when fault could lie elsewhere.

To this point, the story involves a guest in a white gown and an *alleged* clumsy waiter. But what if we had more information—like the waiter tripped over the handbag of a guest at a nearby table? Or the waiter was pushed from behind by a playful co-worker? Or the woman stood up without notice and collided with the waiter? Does this change the nature of the social interaction, our interpretation of the incident, or our assessment of the fault line? In most cases, the answer is "yes" and this is how the imagined, implied, or actual presence of others shapes how common knowledge operates.

This may also explain why the waiter was compelled to declare the obvious— because technically it's not so obvious at all. He admits that it was his fault so she knows that he *already* knows what she already knows and needs him to know: that he is at fault. And his simple admission actually does a lot by ruling out other causal factors. In short, he admits fault so she knows that he knows that, save other factors (e.g., social interactions with nearby guests or playful co-workers), he is the cause of their negative social interaction, knows and *accepts* fault for why her new dress is ruined with tasty gravy, and stands ready to discuss what must be done to rectify the situation. Social influence can be simple and common knowledge can be subtle, yet profound when analyzed carefully. Social psychology and the theories covered in this volume are useful tools for this exercise. QUESTIONS: (1) How can you apply this fictitious scenario or metaphor to higher education? (2) Are there times when "gravy is spilled" and times when we admit fault to students or vice versa? (Those who work in residence life, student conduct, financial aid, or paternity life . . . take it away!)

WHAT'S SOCIAL PSYCHOLOGY?

Social psychology deploys scientific methods to understand and explain how the thoughts, feelings, and behaviors of individuals are influenced by the actual, imagined, or implied presence of others (Allport, 1985). While many other definitions exist, this is perhaps one of the most frequently cited and easy to apprehend.

Social psychology is often considered the study of the obvious or "commonsense." Commonsense, however, may be reduced to nonsense when the validity of such claims are evaluated through theory and research. As an approach, social psychology casts a critical gaze on the individual's subjective evaluation or interpretation of the world around them and how one's behaviors are shaped by others.

WHAT'S SOCIAL INFLUENCE?

As an essential aspect of social psychology, social influence refers to the change in behavior that one person causes in another, intentionally or unintentionally, as a result of the way Person B perceives themselves in relation to Person A, other people, and society in general (Asch, 1946, 1966). Figure 10.1 presents a graphical representation of this dynamic in social settings.

There are three mechanisms through which social influence operates: (a) conformity, (b) compliance, and (c) obedience. **Conformity** generally refers to changing how one behaves to be more like others; in many ways, it plays to belongingness and esteem needs as individuals seek social acceptance, approval, and friends. Prior studies suggest that people will even change beliefs and values to be more like peers.

Conformity is not all bad—we need conformity as a democratic society governed by laws and policies. Imagine a world where everyone raged against conformity at all costs, even when driving on two-lane roads, running for public office, or shopping in the grocery store. Some degree of conformity is required to live peacefully (and without violent accidents) in society.

Compliance is doing what someone else asks you to do. When such a challenge has been placed, the individual might comply or not comply; choices or options are available to them. The ultimate decision to comply or not is influenced by myriad factors including social influences, rewards, incentives, and/or punishment. The image in Figure 10.2 says it all—noncompliance is dangerous and life-threatening in some settings.

Many compliance examples abound. For instance, some schools operate on a compliance model where teachers ask students to sit quietly in their seats or walk in a single-file line. Students have a decision to make—to comply and stand to gain rewards, praise,

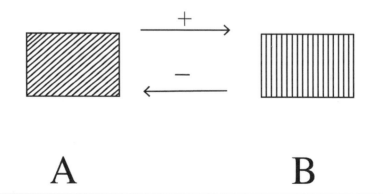

Figure 10.1 Schematic of Social Influence

Figure 10.2 Compliance on the Road

or teacher support or not to comply and reap punishment, correction, or teacher disappointment. Sometimes the student's decision is influenced by the perceived value of the reward offered (monetary reward or free time tend to carry more weight than mere teacher's praise) or whether the social reverence that they might receive from peers for *noncompliance* outweighs the value of other rewards.

Obedience differs from compliance in its relation to authority; obedience is doing something or obeying an order from someone accepted as an authority figure. Authority figures may include parents, guardians, teachers, policemen or correctional officers, to name a few. Individuals are influenced socially by those with authority and choose to obey (or not) by enacting (or avoiding) the desired or expected behavior(s). Obeying those in authority may encouraged through reward, coercion, incentives, and use (or abuse) of legitimate power (Asch, 1966). If social influence is about change in behavior that one person causes in another as a result of the way one perceives themselves in relation to the other person, then obedience as social influence refers to behavioral changes caused in one due to the authority of another. When a police officer demands for one to drop their weapon, this is usually not an invitation to conform or a time to consider compliance or noncompliance; rather it's the use of power and authority to demand obedience. The consequences of not obeying can be grave. See Figure 10.3 for a useful illustration of this point and distinctions between conformity, compliance, and obedience.

Obedience is related to many concepts in student development. For instance, several cognitive-structural theories posit intellectual development as movement from dualist, fundamental ways of knowing (e.g., seeing all things as black or white, right or wrong)

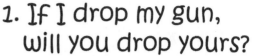

1. If I drop my gun, will you drop yours?

2. If you don't have a license, you cant have a gun.

3. Freeze & drop your gun!

Figure 10.3 The statements articulate distinctions between conformity, compliance, and obedience, respectively

to evaluating, interpreting, and organizing information in more complex ways. Baxter Magolda's (2001) self-authorship theory explains development as a shift from cognitive dissonance to internal foundations by way of becoming author of one's life. It all begins at the *Crossroads*.

Crossroads refers to a point, a place where an individual is in need of self-definition after experiencing rather intense dissonance. Students in this case find their current scripts or ways of knowing inadequate for current challenges or circumstances. They feel hard pressed to consider their own beliefs and to balance them up against others' needs. Quite often the crossroads experience involves looking for affirmation and acceptance.

When one moves from experiencing dissonance or cognitive inadequacy to actively developing perspectives and self-definition they start to become author of their life. Still they will eventually experience conflict between what *they want or believe* (i.e., internal commitments) and external influences. In the end, the individual emerges self-authored, having a set of internally defined perspectives to guide actions and knowledge. *Keep in mind, friends, that encountering perspectives that are new and different causes the cognitive dissonance that is required to catalyze search for new ways of knowing.*

> Change is "induced largely by stimuli arising either from the person's bodily functions or from [their] social and cultural environment."
> —Nevitt Sanford
> (1962, p. 258)

An example is in order. Consider a low-income college student, formerly in foster care, whose adopted parents want her to become a medical doctor. The messages have been all but subtle. For her 10th birthday, they bought her a fake stethoscope, a plastic toy medical bag, and the now-vintage game "Operation." By 15, she had moved to a real stethoscope, a fairly elaborate home microscope, and an all-expenses-paid trip to a summer medical program at a nearby hospital. She enrolled in college "aspiring" to be a medical doctor. By sophomore year, however, she volunteered at a local school and was convinced of the powerful role that teachers can play in students' lives. She realized that much of her own academic success could be attributed to *master teachers* who pushed her to think critically, motivated her to learn, and nurtured her interests in science. Having never thought about teaching as a profession, herself as an educator, or anything other than medicine, she experienced cognitive dissonance marked by questions such as: What's going on with me? How can I change plans now? Where did the idea of pursuing an MD come from? How will I ever tell my parents? Although it is clear that complying with or obeying her parents' wishes would have been the path of least resistance, it would also deny her pursuit of what she's *really interested in*. Committed to the emerging new goal, she changes her major, switches out of the pre-med track, and finds the strength to tell her parents that she aspires to be a teacher.

A QUICK EXERCISE

Thinking about the anecdote of the low-income foster student above, respond to the following questions using information covered in the book to this point.

1. How does this change relate to social psychology, in your own words?
2. What was the role of others in shaping or influencing her decisions regarding a career and major?
3. Which form of social influence most closely relates to the parents' role in the vignette?

AN ACTIVITY

Using Fashion to Fit In

Claire identifies as a pansexual feminist but adopts the label "lesbian" as a way of aligning with other gay, lesbian, bisexual, and transgender (GLBT) students on campus and avoiding what she calls "the conversation"—basically constantly educating others about pansexuality. As a college freshman (although she prefers "freshwmyn"), there are times when she feels alone and desires friends.

An older friend back home advises her to find a gay bar near campus—"there will be plenty of gay college students there and you can find friends." Claire does exactly as advised. Her first night out she notices that lots of gay students have a more eclectic style of dress that is a way more colorful and artsy than her preferred black-on-black or black-and-white designer combinations. The next day she rushes to the mall to buy clothes similar to those that her *would-be friends* sported at the club last night.

Answer the following questions based on information presented in the chapter thus far:

1. Thinking about Claire's decision to follow the advice of an older friend, what form of social influence is best characterized in the story?
2. Define that form of social influence in your own words.
3. Thinking about Claire's decision to change her style, what form of social influence does this best represent?
4. Define that form of social influence in your own words.
5. What if another student led Claire to believe that she would need to change her style of dress to make friends at college? Would that change the form of social influence represented in the story? How and in what way?
6. How does this scenario relate to aspects of belonging, discussed in Chapter 4 of this book?

PERSUASION: A FOURTH FORM OF INFLUENCE

Some authors have advanced a fourth mechanism of social influence—persuasion— although I see persuasion as another form of social influence, deeply connected to the three mechanisms already mentioned. Research, to date, identifies six principles of persuasion:

1. Reciprocation or the reciprocity norm.
2. Consistency or the amplification hypothesis.
3. Social proof or mimicking.
4. Liking and likeability.
5. Authority.
6. Scarcity or the scarcity principle.

As you can see, several principles of persuasion are closely related to dimensions of compliance, conformity, and obedience. For instance, authority refers to being persuaded by those deemed as authorities, which is synonymous with obedience. The "likeability factor" also aligns with issues of social acceptance and belonging within conformity. Still, I think students of social psychology in higher education should understand social influence and how certain behaviors can be brought about or encouraged through persuasion (verbal or non-verbal).

Persuasion works in a number of ways—we are persuaded by those we deem as authorities (principle #5), those we like or want to be liked by (principle #4), or those in close proximity or with whom we compete (principle #3). Persuasion also works through consistency or what many call the "amplification hypothesis" (principle 2). Consider the following conversation between a student and advisor:

Advisor: What do you intend to declare as your academic major?
Student: I have no idea. That's a hard question. There are too many options.
Advisor: What's really important to you in terms of your long-term goals?
Student: I want to work in a field where I can help people and make a difference. Money matters but leaving a mark is what I want.
Advisor: Have you ever thought about social work? Social workers always report enjoying their job. Many get lots of awards and rewards for helping others.
Student: That sounds interesting. But I want to work with young people.
Advisor: Lots of social workers work with youth and make fairly decent money doing so.
Student: Really?! I'm going to look into social work this afternoon as a major. I don't want to take a lot of math classes either. I don't do well in math.
Advisor: Beyond general education requirements, social work majors are not required to take higher level math courses.
Student: OMG . . . really?! Ok, that's my major . . . it's perfect for me.

How did the advisor, knowingly or unknowingly, convince or persuade the student to consider a major in social work? Through verbal persuasion and the principle of consistency, aligning the behavior with the individual's goals and priorities. Study this section until you understand how persuasion and consistency relate to the advisor–student conversation so that you can apply and use it in your work with students too.

AN ACTIVITY

We Do What We Like

A long line of research confirms that attitudes are causally linked to behaviors (Bentler & Speckart, 1981). To illustrate this point, rate the following activities based on your current attitudes, feelings, and thoughts about them:

Activity	5-Very Interested/ Ready to Go	4	3	2	1-Not at all Interested/ Don't Want to Do It
1. Do math					
2. Cook dinner					
3. Run a marathon					
4. Clean the house					
5. Mow the lawn					

Now, rescore the items using the following statements to guide your attitudes, feelings, and thoughts about each activity:

Activity	5-Very Interested/ Ready to Go	4	3	2	1-Not at all Interested/ Don't Want to Do It
1. You love math; do math.					
2. Cooking is messy and takes too much time; cook dinner.					
3. Running is your hobby and therapy; run a marathon.					
4. Chores are thankless tasks; clean the house.					
5. It's hot out and you don't enjoy yardwork; mow the lawn.					

If your scores on #1 and #3 are 3, 4, or 5 *and* your scores on #2, #4, and #5 are 3 or below, then you can see how attitudes (which can be socially cued or provoked) are causally linked to behaviors.

JUST SOCIAL INFLUENCE? A CASE FOR INCENTIVES

Naturally occurring social influence is not the only path for producing changed behavior. There is fairly consistent evidence that financial incentives can work to motivate change too. Financial incentives refer to offering monetary rewards in exchange for engaging in a behavior or accomplishing a particular goal. The weight of empirical evidence suggests that incentives work to change behavior, increase achievement, or enhance performance under certain conditions but not all (Condly, Clark, & Stolovitch, 2003).

Read van Laar Levin, Sinclair, and Sidanius's (2005) study examining the influence of roommate contact on ethnic attitudes and behaviors for college students. Reflective questions: (1) How does this study relate to social psychology? (2) What are the author's main results? (3) How might housing and residence life personnel use this information in their work with students?

Two baseline conditions for incentives to work effectively are that individuals must (a) possess the knowledge, skills, and abilities to complete or perform the incentivized behavior and (b) have the resources and opportunities to complete or perform the incentivized behavior. Similarly incentives should target behaviors that would otherwise not occur, be used repeatedly, be delivered or presented immediately after the incentivized behavior occurs, and be made meaningful to the population (i.e., appropriate for one's age, role, culture). Similar wisdom holds for anyone trying to potty-train a new puppy or teach them how to "roll over, sit, play dead."

Beyond these baseline conditions, incentives need to meet the particular obstacles that individuals face. For instance, financial incentives might be used not only to encourage college students to study abroad but also to help offset the costs associated with doing so. As another example, incentives should be used to encourage the activities necessary to increase math skills and to discourage those that inhibit the development of those skills. Students can be incentivized monetarily for meeting with a teacher, paying attention in class, or going to after-school tutoring, rather than for improving their grade on their own.

Prior research on the effectiveness of financial incentives is mixed. Some studies have consistently demonstrated that financial incentives through performance-based scholarships improve disadvantaged students' performance in terms of grade point average, degree completion, test scores, and college attendance (Jackson, 2010; Pallais, 2009). Yet, not all financial incentive programs produce desirable results over time. For instance, the effects of incentives seem to disappear once the incentives are removed (Fryer, 2011).

BENEFITS OF SOCIAL INFLUENCE: SOCIAL CAPITAL

To this point in the chapter, we've covered several major themes of social psychology and the essential elements of social influence. For example, social influence can lead to changed behavior. Social influence refers to the change in behavior that one person causes in another, intentionally or unintentionally, as a result of the way Person B perceives themselves in relation to Person A, other people, and society in general (Asch, 1946, 1966). Of course, social influence can lead to other outcomes such as resistance to change, maintenance or reinforcement of present behaviors, or a blend of these. Forms of social influence vary, including compliance, conformity, obedience, and persuasion. The underlying causal mechanism for the role that social factors and social interactions play on individuals is multifaceted and complex. So, too, are the penalties and rewards or benefits that flow to those who are influenced one way or another.

One way we understand the benefits that accrue to individuals through social influence is known as social capital. Social capital is related to and informed by human capital theory (Becker, 1993). Human capital suggests that individuals make investments in education and training, thereby gaining knowledge, skills, and abilities that are often exchanged or traded in the labor market for increased likelihood of employment, earnings, job status, and economic success. Generally, the more education an individual attains, the more human capital one accumulates and can use for monetary and non-monetary returns.

Like human capital, social capital is a resource that can be invested to enhance profitability, increase productivity, and facilitate upward social mobility (Lamont & Lareau, 1988). Social capital takes the form of information-sharing networks as well as social norms, values, and expected behaviors. It also refers to the way in which these connections are maintained (Strayhorn, 2008). One way social capital may influence or benefit one's outcomes is through provision of specialized knowledge and information. It may also relate to one's values and preferences about education and the value of obtaining a college degree.

Social capital has been examined in relation to many topics in higher education. For example, dozens of studies have explored the association between social capital and parental involvement and support (Kim & Schneider, 2005; McNeal, 1999; Perna & Titus, 2005). Others have studied family–school relationships (Lareau, 1987) and college decisions of students of color (Perna, 2000; Strayhorn, 2010), to name a few. Similar to what we covered in the chapter on ecological systems theory, research has shown that campus environments or contexts shape social capital networks and students' experiences (Palmer & Gasman, 2008). If nothing else, we know from research that students' educational aspirations can be influenced by others such as parents, teachers, peers, and media messages. Sometimes messages about the value of a college education or the importance of a college degree are transmitted through the social capital networks of students and families.

CONNECTING THE DOTS: SOCIAL INFLUENCE AND EDUCATIONAL ASPIRATIONS

Carter (2001) pointed out "the controversy and confusion with respect to the measurement of aspirations and expectations" (p. 11). The two terms are often used synonymously but have been operationalized in myriad ways (Adelman, 1999). For example, aspiration is defined in most dictionaries as a strong aim, desire, or ambition—a goal that may be hoped for, even in the face of evidence that suggests it may be beyond one's ability or expectation. A classic way of assessing one's educational aspirations is: "By age 30, what level of education do you hope to hold?" Response options usually range from "high school diploma" to "doctoral degree or first professional degree (MD, JD)."

Expectations, on the other hand, are defined as mental attitudes that reflect what one thinks as generally possible or feasible, in light of certain abilities, constraints, or realities. Educational expectations reflect the degree of probability that one might attain a certain level of education within a particular period of time, given a realistic assessment of the state of affairs including academic ability, finances, past performance, social contexts, and even the likelihood that a student will invest the time that it takes to complete higher levels of education. A classic way of assessing one's educational expectations is: "What is the highest level of education that you expect to attain in your lifetime?" Sometimes to remove the effect of social class differences, surveys might ask: "Barring finances and the costs of college, what is the highest level of education that you *expect* to complete in your lifetime?" Response options are placed on the same range as mentioned above.

Much of what we have discussed in this chapter attempts to connect social psychology generally and social influence specifically to educational aspirations. One mechanism through which this occurs is social capital. Imagine a student, Wilmar, who grows up on the Southside of Chicago and attends a private, selective academy. His parents, both first-generation to the United States from Cuba, work white-collar jobs and direct a good deal of attention to their son's education. They're actively involved in his education and have strong records of attending parent–teacher conferences, monitoring his homework, and cultivating his interests in piano, swimming, and volunteerism through after-school activities.

Though first-generation, they work with several very successful individuals whose academic pedigree can be traced to places like Harvard, Yale, Duke, Stanford, Virginia, and a few of the "Big Ten." They have kids who *aspire* (and *expect*) to attend college one day; in fact, most of them spend lots of time talking about college applications, college tours, and how to maximize their summers through camps, clubs, overseas vacations, and SAT prep courses. The two Cuban parents learn a lot from their friends at work and share that information with Wilmar to set him up for success in college too. Just last summer they took their first college visit to the University of Chicago, Vanderbilt

University, and The Ohio State University. Wilmar was even more inspired (or should we say *aspired*) to attend college one day.

Before moving to the next section, answer the following questions as a way of reviewing information from the chapter:

1. How is the story about Wilmar an illustration of social capital?
2. How is the story about Wilmar, especially Wilmar's parents, an illustration of social influence?
3. In what way, if any, do you see the story as a characterization of *conformity*?
4. In what way, if any, do you see the story as a characterization of *compliance*?
5. How might the story be recast or modified to represent an example of *obedience*?
6. Look back at the section on *persuasion*, identify one of the core elements that relates to an aspect of Wilmar's story, and explain your choice.

Linking Identity Development to Social Influence

Think back to student development theory. Students of higher education and student affairs will be familiar with Chickering's (1969) Seven Vectors. Chickering posits identity development as progress through multiple vectors, hierarchically organized, revealing shifts in ways of thinking, being, and behaving largely during college years or late adolescence. The seven vectors include:

1. Developing competence.
2. Managing emotions.
3. Moving through autonomy toward interdependence.
4. Developing mature interpersonal relationships.
5. Establishing identity.
6. Developing purpose.
7. Developing integrity.

While not always so explicitly framed, Chickering's theory relates to our discussion of social psychology and the social influence of others on human attitudes and behaviors. Let's consider the 5th vector, *establishing identity*. Prior research defines this vector as involving comfort with bodily appearance, comfort with gender and sexual orientation, sense of self in a social, historical, and cultural context and sense of self in response to feedback from valued others. Experimentation is essential to this process and ultimately the vector is characterized by progress to seeing one's core self as worthy.

Now thinking about what's been covered, respond to the following questions:

1. How do others play a role in *establishing identity*?
2. Are others and self always mutually exclusive? Offer a few examples to support your point.
3. How is the "establishing identity" vector shaped by the implied, imagined, or actual presence of others?

A POP QUIZ

1. What's social psychology, in your own words?
2. List at least three main points that you take away from the book.
3. Define social capital in your own words.
4. What's the difference between educational aspirations and expectations?

THEORY TO PRACTICE: A CASE STUDY

A Tale of One City

Vincent and Terrance were born in Kalamazoo, Michigan. Vincent identifies as Asian American, "part Chinese and part Vietnamese to be exact." Terrance identifies as African American and prefers to use "Black" as a racial identity label. Interestingly, both stand at approximately 5 feet, 8 inches, medium build. Neither particularly athletic nor musical, but both industrious and hardworking. Vincent aspires to be an engineer and hopes to attend Michigan State University (MSU) to major in mechanical engineering. Terrance, on the other hand, "knows [he] hopes to attend college" but is unsure of his intended major and career interest.

Vincent has long admired MSU and knows quite a bit about the institution thanks to first-hand insights from his parents' friends who are MSU alumni. In fact, his Aunt Priscilla (his dad's sister) also attended MSU and presents Vincent with MSU paraphernalia from time-to-time during holidays and birthdays. One year, an MSU baseball cap. Another year an MSU mousepad, pen, and padfolio. Like most kids, Vincent has lost or destroyed many toys over the years; but, his MSU gifts from Aunt Priscilla remain his most prized and protected.

When it comes time to apply to college, Vincent and Terrance unknowingly both apply to MSU. Vincent is admitted. Terrance is not. How can we explain these differences in admission outcomes? Apart from academic readiness for college, social capital, social influence, and aspirations play an important role in this process. Now, let's consider the following:

1. How does the story relate to social capital?
2. How does the story relate to social influence?
3. Who are the social influences in Vincent's life? What about Terrance?
4. Theorize about the college admission outcomes of each student by completing the following phrases: "Using social psychological theory as a guide, I hypothesize that Vincent's college admission is likely due to . . ." and then "Using social psychological theory as a guide, I hypothesize that Terrance's rejection decision is likely due to . . ."

A MOMENT TO REFLECT

Use the following scales to indicate the highest level of education that one *aspires* or hopes to attain in their lifetime. In cases where you do NOT know, contact the person via any media (e.g., email, text, social network) and ask—*do not guess.*

Now compare responses across the chart:

	High school diploma	Associate's degree	Bachelor's degree	Master's degree	Doctorate or JD, MD
YOU					
Your best friend					
A person sitting nearby					
One of your mentors					
A kid you know under age 12					

1. What trends do you notice?
2. What surprises you most?
3. How do you think each person's response is socially influenced?

A CLOSING ACTIVITY

Respond to the following questions with "True" or "False." When completed, discuss your answers first in a small group (no more than four people per group) and then in a larger group or full class discussion.

ITEM	TRUE	FALSE
1. Focusing on a person's voice versus their facial expression is a better way to detect whether they're lying.		
2. Seeing a picture of a person from a stereotyped group for very few seconds can trigger thoughts of the stereotype.		
3. Once people reject a larger request, they are more likely to agree to a smaller request.		
4. Physically attractive people are usually assumed more intelligent than ugly people.		
5. "Birds of a feather flock together."		
6. Very wealthy people are happier than most other people.		
7. People with lots of friends live longer and are healthier than those with few friends.		
8. Putting on a happy face will not make you feel better, more positive.		

Answer Key: [1] False; facial is better detector; [2] True; takes little time; [3] True; keep this in mind when negotiating job offers—aim high; [4] True, but there is no association between physical beauty and IQ; [5] True; [6] False; [7] True; so make friends today; [8] False; it will, so smile before proceeding to the next section.

THEORY TO PRACTICE: A CASE STUDY

It's Wednesday. You just finished a stressful staff meeting marked by heated debate about the role that student affairs professionals play in the academic mission of the university. Your opinion—that student affairs professionals are *equal* partners with staff within academic affairs and other units on campus—was in the numerical and "vocal" minority. Right now, you're wondering if your colleagues outside of student affairs see any value to your presence on campus (beyond graduated babysitting and "doing fun stuff with students," as one mentioned in the meeting).

Annoyed and confused, you speak to your supervisor about your frustrations, realize she shares your concerns, and she offers you an opportunity to address the group at next week's joint staff meeting. Nervous but convinced that you may have the capacity to convince or *persuade* your academic colleagues to see value in what student affairs contributes to achievement of the academic mission, you sit down to develop a strategy.

Fortunately you still have your notes from the social psychological theory course you took in graduate school. You turn quickly to the chapter and unit on social influence. It's all coming back to you now—imagined, implied, compliance, conformity, persuasion, and social capital as examples.

Complete the matrix shown in Figure 10.4 to outline a strategy for your directed conversation with the group.

CONCLUSION

This chapter closes by circling back to how it began. We started with my open admission that this chapter was added to the line up or table of contents long after I thought the book was done. Candid conversations with students, friends, publishers, and my own thoughts about social psychological phenomena revealed the importance of explicitly covering the role that social influence plays on human behavior and the possibility of using educational aspirations as the connecting point. Now, many pages later, I realize that I had quite a bit to say about the topic after all.

Question to Consider	*Your Response*
What's the main point you want to make to your academic colleagues?	
Which form of social influence holds the most promise for achieving your purpose?	
What role, if any, might persuasion play in your strategy? Name specific principles.	
What role can your supervisor or the senior student affairs officer play and how does it relate to social influence?	
What are your concerns, if any, in facing the group next week?	

Figure 10.4

A few points deserve repeating in a concluding section on social influence. Humans are powerfully influenced by those around them and the prevailing literature suggests that social influence occurs through conformity, compliance, obedience, and persuasion. Persuasion has several principles such as reciprocation, consistency, mimicking, likeability, and authority, some of which are closely related to the primary three sources of influence.

Social change can be provoked through the use of authority, financial incentives, and multiple forms of influence. One way in which we talk about the benefits of social influence is through social capital theory. Social capital, related to human capital, refers to resource- or information-rich, productive networks and relationships through which the individual acquires knowledge, skills, information that can be exchanged, traded, or sold in the market for personal gain, monetary or nonmonetary reward, or collective advancement of a group or family.

Lastly, despite relatively frequent interchangeable use, educational *aspirations* and *expectations* are not equal. Aspirations refers to one's strong aim, desire, or ambition—a goal that may be hoped for, even in the face of evidence that suggests it may be beyond one's ability or expectation. Expectations, on the other hand, are defined as mental attitudes that reflect what one thinks as generally possible or feasible, in light of certain abilities, constraints, or realities. In short, it is possible for students to aspire to attain a master's degree although they *expect* to stop after high school graduation given certain constraints and limits. For instance, I once interviewed a student who shared that he hoped to earn a masters degree but expected to complete high school, in light of the fact that most men "in his neighbourhood" didn't live beyond age 20 "on the streets where he [sic] from," quoted in his own voice.

REFLECTIVE EXERCISES

1. Define social psychology. (You should be a pro at this by now.)
2. Define social influence.
3. What's the difference between compliance and conformity, if any?
4. List and briefly define one principle of persuasion.
5. What is your primary take-away from this chapter? Name up to three.
6. *To Go to Class or Not: That is the Question.* Kevion is a biology major, philosophy minor at a highly selective four-year predominantly White institution located in the Midwest region of the country. Today, he has class lecture for microbiology and his philosophy professor is showing a video titled, "Black Matter" that raises issues such as global warming, euthanasia, and eugenics. It's clear that this material will be on the final exam. On his way to class, books and notes in tow, Kevion runs into his friend, Nathaniel (people call him "Nate" for short). "Hey, you want to join me, Chris, and Xavier for a few games of 2-on-2 basketball . . . we're about to shoot hoops real quick, but we need one more person," Nate asked. Then pleaded. Then begged. After several exchanges that started with Kevion saying, "No, I've got class," the conversation evolved into him saying, "Ok, well maybe so man" and skipping class to go play ball. *Answer the following questions using information from the chapter*: (a) What form of social influence is best reflected in the scenario? (b) Define that type of social influence in your own words. (c) What role does Nate play in the social influence? (d) Imagine advising Kevion about the importance of class attendance. He tells you about the frequent occurrence of being derailed from class by friends. List at least three things Kevion can do to manage that conversation

differently in the future and how do your suggested strategies relate to social influence theory? (e) How can you acquire information about Kevion's aspirations and use it to help him develop a strategy that will lead to academic success?

CHAPTER SUMMARY

1. Human are powerfully influenced by others.
2. The magnitude of that influence is determined, at least in part, by a host of social factors (e.g., proximity) and the nature of their social connection to one another.
3. There are three mechanisms through which social influence operates: (a) conformity, (b) compliance, and (c) obedience.
4. A fourth mechanism through which social influence operates is persuasion.
5. Persuasion has six key principles: reciprocation, consistency, likeability, mimicking, authority, and scarcity.
6. Cognitive dissonance or inadequacy is a necessary but insufficient condition for optimal learning.
7. Attitudes are causally linked to behaviors.
8. Incentives are another way of encouraging or influencing human behaviors.
9. Social capital is related to and informed by human capital theory. Social capital is a resource that can be invested to enhance profitability, increase productivity, and facilitate upward social mobility.
10. Aspirations ≠ Expectations.

DEFINITIONS

Use a dictionary to define the following terms or concepts that relate to social influence:

aspirations
expectations
goals
identity development
motivation
self-authorship
social capital
social influence
social psychology
crossroads
conformity
compliance
obedience

RESEARCH TIPS

1. Relatively little research exists in higher education on the outcomes of multiple mechanisms for social influence. Future studies might use both quantitative and qualitative methods to discern the influence of conformity, compliance, and obedience on college students' behaviors.

2. Social capital theory supports framing it as a resource that can be invested, exchanged, even traded for profit. But there may be evidence that not all social capital networks are the same, neither do they necessarily operate equally. Future research should be designed to unearth such differences and provide keen insights into what that means for educational practice.

FURTHER READING

Alexander, K. L., & Cook, M. A. (1979). The motivational relevance of educational plans: Questioning the conventional wisdom. *Social Psychology Quarterly, 42*(3), 202–213.

Crocker, J., Karpinski, A., Quinn, D. M., & Chase, S. K. (2003). When grades determine self-worth: Consequences of contingent self-worth for male and female engineering and psychology majors. *Journal of Personality and Social Psychology, 85*, 507–516.

Johnson, J. D., Adams, M. S., Ashburn, L., & Reed, W. (1995). Differential gender effects of exposure to rap music on African American adolescents' acceptance of teen dating violence. *Sex Roles, 33*, 597–605.

Khattab, N. (2005). The effects of high school context and interpersonal factors on students' educational expectations: A multi-level model. *Social Psychology of Education, 8*, 19–40.

REFERENCES

Adelman, C. (1999*). Answers in the toolbox: Academic intensity, attendance patterns, and bachelor's degree attainment.* Washington, DC: U.S. Department of Education, Office of Educational Research and Improvement.

Allport, G. W. (1985). The historical background of social psychology. In G. Lindzey & E. Aronson (Eds.), *Handbook of Social Psychology* (Vol. 1, pp. 1–46). New York: Random House.

Asch, S. E. (1946). Forming impressions of personality. *Journal of Abnormal and Social Psychology, 41*, 258–290.

Asch, S. E. (1966). Opinions and social pressure. In A. P. Hare, E. F. Borgatta, & R. F. Bales (Eds.), *Small groups: Studies in social interacton* (pp. 318–324). New York: Alfred A. Knopf.

Baxter Magolda, M. B. (2001). *Making their own way: Narratives for transforming higher education to promote self-development.* Sterling, VA: Stylus.

Becker, G. S. (1993). *Human capital: A theoretical and empirical analysis with special reference to education.* Chicago, IL: University of Chicago Press.

Bentler, P. M., & Speckart, G. (1981). Attitudes "cause" behaviors: A structural equation analysis. *Journal of Personality and Social Psychology, 40*(2), 226–238.

Carter, D. F. (2001). *A dream deferred? Examining the degree aspirations of African American and White college students.* New York: RoutledgeFalmer.

Chickering, A. W. (1969). *Education and identity.* San Francisco, CA: Jossey-Bass.

Condly, S. J., Clark, R. E., & Stolovitch, H. D. (2003). The effects of incentives on workplace performance: A meta-analytic review of research studies. *Performance Improvement Quarterly, 16*, 46–63.

Fryer, R. G. (2011). Financial incentives and student achievement: Evidence from randomized trials. *The Quarterly Journal of Economics, 126*, 1755–1798.

Hume, D. (1740). *A treatise of human nature.* Oxford: Oxford University Press.

Jackson, C. K. (2010). A little now for a lot later: A look at a Texas Advanced Placement incentive program. *Journal of Human Resources, 45*, 591–639.

Kim, D. H., & Schneider, B. (2005). Social capital in action: Alignment of parental support in adolescents' transition to postsecondary education. *Social Forces, 84*(2), 1181–1206.

Lamont, M., & Lareau, A. (1988). Cultural capital: Allusions, gaps, and glissandos in recent theoretical developments. *Sociological Theory, 6*, 153–168.

Lareau, A. (1987). Social class differences in family-school relationships: The importance of cultural capital. *Sociology of Education, 60*, 73–85.

Lewis, D. (1969). *Convention: A philosophical study.* Cambridge, MA: Harvard University Press.

McNeal, R. B. (1999). Parental involvement as social capital: Differential effectiveness on science, achievement, truancy, and dropping out. *Social Forces, 78*, 117–144.

Pallais, A. (2009). Taking a chance on college: Is the Tennessee Education Lottery Scholarship a winner? *Journal of Human Resources, 44*, 199–222.

Palmer, R. T., & Gasman, M. B. (2008). "It takes a village to raise a child": The role of social capital in promoting academic success of African American men at a Black college. *Journal of College Student Development, 49*(1), 52–70.

Perna, L. W. (2000). Differences in the decision to attend college among African Americans, Hispanics, and Whites. *The Journal of Higher Education, 71*(2), 117–141.

Perna, L. W., & Titus, M. A. (2005). The relationship between parental involvement as social capital and college enrollment: An examination of racial/group differences. *Journal of Higher Education, 76*, 486–518.

Sanford, N. (1962). Developmental status of the entering freshman. In N. Sanford (Ed.), *The American college* (pp. 253–282). New York: Wiley.

Strayhorn, T. L. (2008). Influences on labor market outcomes of African American college graduates: A national study. *The Journal of Higher Education, 79*(1), 29–57.

Strayhorn, T. L. (2010). When race and gender collide: The impact of social and cultural capital on the academic achievement of African American and Latino males. *The Review of Higher Education, 33*(3), 307–332.

Strayhorn, T. L. (2011). Singing in a foreign land: An exploratory study of gospel choir participation among African American undergraduates at a predominantly White institution. *Journal of College Student Development, 52*(5), 137–153.

van Laar, C., Levin, S., Sinclair, S., & Sidanius, J. (2005). The effect of university roommate contact on ethnic attitudes and behavior. *Journal of Experimental Social Psychology, 41*, 329–345.

11

EPILOGUE

"All good things must come to an end," as the saying goes. After over two years of hard work, this book too must end with this chapter. We've covered a lot of ground with respect to social psychological theory in higher education and educational practice in both academic and student affairs. In this chapter, we will review the book's purpose, review its organization, highlight key points from selected chapters, and then move to a discussion of broader implications.

Recall the book's main purposes. First, the book is a textbook and has a strong instructional thrust for that reason. The inclusion of quizzes, learning exercises, reflective activities, and vignettes reflects that objective. Second, the book aimed to synthesize, not merely review, information related to the theory that is the focus of a particular chapter. In this way, the book was designed to provide readers with an appropriate introduction to in-depth discussion of theory. Synthesis of major theoretical threads and conceptual components was used to enhance readers' understanding of social psychological concepts. New models and figures were developed and included in the book for this reason.

Another purpose of the book was to maximize students' learning and development of understanding about social psychological theory in higher education. For this reason and more, several other signature components were included to enhance pedagogical effectiveness. These range from summary material at the end of each chapter to guiding questions, research tips to further reading lists. Some chapters include extensive shaded boxes or "call outs" that share detailed information about methodological approaches such as narrative inquiry or historical facts about theorists. A collection of tables, figures, and images also illustrate points raised in various chapters.

THE BOOK IN REVIEW

Student Development in Higher Education: A Social Psychological Perspective is organized into 10 substantive chapters. Chapter 1 serves as the book's introduction to the fields of social psychology. Chapter 2 takes up the all-too-important issue of theory and its utility in higher education research and practice. Chapters 3 through 10 each focus on various social psychological theories including, but not limited to, ecological systems theory, sense of belonging, grit, and hope. This discussion (Chapter 11) serves as the book's epilogue.

Some chapters engage a topic about which much is written in higher education. For instance, in Chapter 4, I revisited a topic to which I have directed much attention over the past few years, namely sense of belonging. Sense of belonging is a basic human need, sufficient to drive behavior. It is related to mattering and mattering has several components: attention, importance, dependence, appreciation, and ego extension.

Consider the following as a final set of exercises regarding belonging from a social psychological perspective:

A Quick Quiz

1. What's social psychology, in your own words?
2. List at least three main points about belonging that you take away from the book.
3. What did you find most compelling about belonging from the book's content?
4. How might you use belonging in your work?
5. What topics related to belonging would you like to investigate further in this course, a future course, or your own time?

Other chapters engage topics that are rarely, if ever, discussed in higher education research. For instance, in Chapter 9, we turned attention to hope theory and a social psychological approach to understanding hope that moves toward knowing how parents, peers, mentors, or spiritual figures influence one's hope for better or more. Hope is generally defined as the perceived ability to clearly conceptualize one's goals and derive paths to achieve them (Snyder, 2002). Hope is a feeling of anticipation, that some desire will be satisfied or a promise will be fulfilled despite delay, setback, or trouble (Snyder, 2000). Hope has three primary components: goals, pathways, and agency. And it has four constitutive elements: mastery, attachment, survival, and spiritual. Mastery, for instance, refers to priorities and feelings of control.

Hope theory has many applications to practice, some of which were discussed in Chapter 9. Recall that Norma Cousins, American journalist, once said: "The capacity for hope is the most significant fact of life. It provides human beings with a sense of destination, and the energy to get started." Indeed, prior research suggests that hope is both an input and output, a means and an end. The same is true in higher education and it is that understanding that we should bring to bear in our work with college students.

Consider the following as a final exercise regarding hope from a social psychological perspective:

1. In 2008, then Senator Barack Obama won the national presidential election on a campaign for hope and change. Many will recall the red, white, and blue Democratic party signs that displayed Barack Obama's cameo under a bold heading of simply "CHANGE" or "HOPE." Why do you think his campaign for hope was so successful? How does your explanation relate to hope theory?

2. Many Americans, especially youth and/or people of color supported Barack Obama's race for the White House by organizing locally, campaigning door-to-door, and doing whatever was needed to spread the word about the hope campaign. One woman shared that she did what she needed to do in her neighborhood because she knew there were other people—men, women, and children—across the country doing the same thing in their area. How does this rationalization relate to social psychology?

3. Consider the following items adapted from Snyder et al.'s "The Hope Scale," and then describe how hope relates to the goals that President Barack Obama likely had in mind for the campaign:

	1	*2*	*3*	*4*	*5*
	Not at all true				*Very true*

a. I am able to rely on others to achieve my goals.
b. I can find lots of ways around any problem.
c. I achieve the goals that I set for myself.

4. In your own words and *regardless of your own political opinion*, how do you think hope relates to President Obama's goals and objectives for the presidential campaign?

It is my hope that this volume has shown that social psychology is a field of study with an expansive literature base, deep theoretical insights, and rigorous methods for inquiry. The scope, structure, and content of social psychology are relevant to higher education. Thus, such theory can elicit the collective consideration of higher education professionals, scientists, and students.

There are substantial research findings and theoretical hypotheses from social psychology that deserve (even invite) investigation. For instance, belonging, grit, prejudice, and stereotypes are significantly useful in our work to ensure student success, enhance teaching and learning environments, retain productive faculty, and build institutional capacity. Yet, as we come to the end of this book one undeniable impression is how much remains to be done.

FUTURE DIRECTIONS

What directions ought new inquiry take? First, we need more effort toward developing new or expanding existing social psychological theories. Personality development is one area where such growth is needed. What's personality? Is personality fixed or malleable, responsive to intervention? To what extent, if any, do these answers apply to college student populations. From time to time in this volume I called attention to the need for such theoretical advancements.

My call for more theory is more than what good higher education writers do. My call for more is fueled both by a sense of what can be achieved if modern theories were formulated (and used effectively in practice) and what results if we continue in the direction of "theorylessness": higher education research or empirical observations increase and we become overwhelmed and the field over-saturated by a sea of disconnected facts.

More than theory or general hypotheses about social psychological phenomena in higher education settings, we would benefit from theory pertaining to social psychological development in late adolescence. This barren area in the field—lack of research informed by such theories—accounts for one of the largest gaps in the college impacts literature. For instance, consider Chapter 3. Here we discussed considerable evidence of change in students through an ecological systems perspective, but when it comes to the question of what makes such change occur there is little to nothing to say. Much more information is needed about the dynamics of social psychological change.

There are several reasons why this call deserves additional mention and explanation, even at the risk of sounding redundant. First, it is precisely knowledge of what determines change (not just the plausibility of change) that is of more value to college student educators. These professionals are often called upon to produce change in students, sometimes quickly without adequate resources. Decisions about who, what, when, where, how, how much, and how frequently (i.e., dosage) are informed by knowledge of change dynamics.

How might we produce the necessary theory? Simple question, complex answer. For starters, we must resist the urge to sit, think, and make theoretical generalizations about college students from observations of children or aging adults, supposing the same holds true for those in late adolescence. The latter has been the dominant thrust of extant research. Higher education researchers and practitioners interested in the dynamics of change for college students must observe them in a variety of settings, on and off campus, then strive to produce social psychological theoretical propositions about what is observed.

Another important point is to keep one's eyes on the prize, so to speak. Those interested in building such theory must recognize that the emergent theory pertains to development—that is, progressive and eventual change over relatively long periods of time—thus the theory-maker must be patient with enduring inquiry. This won't come overnight nor should it. While the investigator certainly benefits from a healthy dose of patience and preparation, they need not recreate the wheel entirely. Tentative formulations and basic postulates already exist. Many of them have been introduced in this book, particularly in Chapters 1 and 3 through 10. All of these stand to be further challenged, confirmed, or replicated. Investigators may find it productive to seek answers to theory-related research questions, test practical hypotheses of existing models, or a blend of both. Either way, researchers are encouraged to pursue their curiosity wherever it leads.

Beyond making theory, there are implications for future research methods and techniques. Suppose a theory-maker had a proposition in mind concerning the conditions that facilitate some kind of developmental change that we desire for students in college. For instance, the modern theorist might suppose that faculty–student collaboration in research promotes ethical decisionmaking or self-efficacy in college students or a particular pattern of experience such as increasing democratic participation or reducing prejudice in college. Confirmation of this proposition can only be achieved through experimental design. True experiments can be difficult to mount in college since granting access for some to an educational intervention (e.g., practice, experience, tool) while denying others is generally illegal, if not just bad publicity in higher education. Even in quasi-experimental design, an impressive set of controls would need to be included to determine with any degree of certainty that the change under question was due to the conditions (i.e., independent variable) rather than other confounding influences. Still, advanced theory, experimental studies, and quasi-experimental work is sorely needed in social psychological higher education research.

One of the most glaring needs is for empirical research that relates to the theory that is now available. For instance, Chapter 4 focuses on sense of belonging. Research is needed that explores belonging for students living with disabilities, veterans, and Muslims, to name a few. Chapter 7 focuses on personality. Future research might explore personality, its origins, malleability, and correlates in higher education. Additional research is needed about such factors as hope, ecological systems, and prejudice, to name a few. The next section continues this discussion beyond a recall of the book's main purposes, organization, and key points to a number of final conclusions.

CONCLUSION

Several currents will drive the shelf-life of this book for those training to be competent, effective higher education professionals. For instance, consider that there are over 21 million individuals enrolled across approximately 4,300 colleges and universities in the United States (U.S. Department of Education, 2013), making it the largest higher education enterprise in the world. The nation's higher education system is marked off from others by the diversity of its institutions and students. Over half of postsecondary institutions are 2-year community colleges that are generally open access (i.e., open admissions or admission guaranteed to any high school graduate) and low cost. A growing sector of the enterprise is for-profit and online schools. In terms of students, today women outnumber men on most college campuses and approximately one-third of all students are first-generation to college. Racial/ethnic minorities constitute a greater proportion of college students nationally than ever before and the average family income for Pell grant recipients is approximately $21,000 per year, well below federal poverty guidelines. Increasing diversity of schools and students will bring new and different questions about development in college, how social interactions are facilitated, and the change that college student educators might expect in such contexts. These questions are addressed in the present volume.

Other forces that will drive the relevance of this book are environmental and social changes such as the advent of emerging technologies. Such changes will shape the nature of social interactions inviting new and different questions about the influence of the actual, imagined, or implied presence of others on human behaviors. As these questions emerge and are identified daily, insights offered in this book may be brought to bear in educational practice. Future editions of the book will extend what is provided to cover unanticipated extensions of fundamental inquiries.

None of the trends mentioned show signs of abating in coming decades, so higher education professionals will continue to face critical challenges and questions in their daily practices. Building the capacity to educate aspiring professionals who are aware of social psychological dimensions of student development (not just typical identity and psychosocial developmental theory) is critical. Continuing to assemble a persuasive body of research and theory is crucial. This book introduces frameworks that can be used to expand discussion of core concepts in higher education.

Despite all that has been written, we are not yet able to promote predetermined forms of student development intentionally on a large or larger scale in higher education. Admittedly it may never be possible to design effective interventions, ensure consistent implementation across multiple sites, classrooms, or majors, or exercise all necessary controls within uncertain, unstable, unpredictable learning environments to achieve such a goal. Still productive steps can be (and have been) taken, drawing upon existing knowledge of theories of development, college impact research, and social psychology. Even on a small scale, promoting student development in higher education, especially in social psychological domains of human behavior, is a tall order.

Chickering and Havighurst (1981) in *The Modern American College* stated: "the idea of human development can supply a unifying purpose for higher education" (p. xxx). That human development, specifically student development, is a "unifying purpose" mutually agreed upon by those working in higher education across both academic and student affairs is far from true, even at the time of this writing, which is over 30 years after Chickering and Havighurst's prescient pronouncement. Faculty hardly agree that their work in the classroom—from classics to math, biology to music appreciation— ought to push students' intellectual capacities as well as their self-awareness, ethical decisionmaking, and spirituality. Those in student affairs are more likely to accept the assignment of raising students' creative energies, clarifying their career interests, and making them fit to work on a team but many struggle to connect experiences in a campus club, band, or sports team to effective communication skills or cognitive complexity (Strayhorn, 2006). Nevertheless, student development broadly conceived is the goal of higher education even in the realm of social psychological changes. An understanding of social psychology as it relates to higher education and student development is crucial to achieving that "unifying purpose" that Chickering and Havighurst spoke of almost prophetically. This book was designed with these points in mind. I hope you agree that it met, if not exceeded, these goals and inspired your interest in learning more. For life is nothing if it is not learning.

REFERENCES

Chickering, A. W., & Havighurst, R. J. (1981). The life cycle. In A. W. Chickering & Associates (Eds.), *The modern American college*. San Francisco, CA: Jossey-Bass.

Snyder, C. R. (Ed.). (2000). *Handbook of hope: Theory, measures, and applications*. New York: Academic Press.

Snyder, C. R. (2002). Hope theory: Rainbows in the mind. *Psychological Inquiry, 13*(4), 249–275.

Strayhorn, T. L. (2006). *Frameworks for assessing learning and development outcomes*. Washington, DC: Council for the Advancement of Standards in Higher Education (CAS).

U.S. Department of Education, National Center for Education Statistics. (2013). *The condition of education 2013*. Washington, DC: U.S. Government Printing Office.

INDEX

Note: Page numbers in **bold** are for figures.